A Guide Book of Experiments

in

Applied Chemistry

Dr. Sapana Gupta
Visiting Faculty, Impedance Academy Raipur
Former Assistant Professor
(Central Institute of Technology, Raipur CG, INDIA)

Dr. V. K. Jena
Assistant Professor
Department of Chemistry
(Government Nagarjuna P. G. College of Science, Raipur CG, INDIA)

LP INC. PUBLISHER NORTH CAROLINA, USA
2017

LP INC. PUBLISHER NORTH CAROLINA, USA

First Printing: 2017

ISBN: 978-1-365-68298-8

PREFACE

We understands the importance of laboratory work in the study of chemistry and committed to educate the student in lab skill and hopes that they will take full advantage of this opportunity. So, it is very important that students of chemistry perform lab experiments to fully understand that the theories they study in lecture and in their textbook are developed from the critical evaluation of experimental data. The laboratory can also help the student to develop interest in the study of the science by clearly illustrating the principles and concepts involved. Finally, laboratory experimentation teaches students the opportunity to develop techniques and other manipulative skills that students of engineering must master for application in career and daily life. This Engineering Chemistry guide book provides the students a clear, comprehensive and up to date information about the various practical of chemistry as applied to engineering chemistry. In addition, students are encouraged to complete the report as soon after laboratory as possible, as this is much more efficient than waiting until the night before it is due. Finally, we hope you find this laboratory manual helpful in your study of chemistry.

Dr. S Gupta
Dr. V. K. Jena
Raipur

CONTENTS

EXPERIMENTS 1

To find out type of alkalinity and estimate alkalinity present in the given water sample.

Chemicals:

Std. Na_2CO_3 solution, Unknown water sample A, HCl solution as an intermediate solution, phenolphthalein indicator and methyl orange/red indicator

Principle:

The alkalinity of a water sample is due to carbonates (CO_3^{2-}), bicarbonates (HCO_3^-) and hydroxide (OH^-) ions. Thus in a given water sample the possible combination of ions causing alkalinity are as follows.

(i) OH^- alone(ii) CO_3^{2-} alone(iii) HCO_3^-alone(iv) OH^- and CO_3^{2-} together(v) CO_3^{2-}-and HCO_3^-together

The possibility of OHand HCO3-ions together in the same solution is ruled out as they react as

$$HCO^- + OH^- \rightarrow CO_3^{2-} + H_2O$$

In the same way, possibility of co -existence of all the three OH-, CO32-and HCO3-is ruled out.

The determination of alkalinity involves following reactions:

$$OH^- + H^+ \longrightarrow H_2O \qquad \text{----------------(1)}$$

$$CO_3^{2-} + H^+ \longrightarrow HCO_3^- \qquad \text{----------------(2)}$$

$$HCO_3^- + H^+ \longrightarrow H_2CO_3 \longrightarrow H_2O + CO_2 \qquad \text{---------------- (3)}$$

The phenolphthalein is pink in color above pH 10 and it is colorless below pH-8. While, the methyl orange is yellow above pH 4.4 and it turns pink below pH 3.1Thus titration of a given water sample in presence of phenolphthalein as an indicator indicates completion of reaction 1 and 2 whereas the same water sample, if titrated in presence of Methyl orange as an indicator indicates the completion of reaction 1, 2 and 3.

he water sample, when titrated with an acid solution using phenolphthalein indicator gives (End point = P) and with methyl orange indicator gives (End point = M). The relation between P and M points gives the type and extent of alkalinity is established as follows:-

Table 1

Relation between P & M	Types of alkalinity	Extent of alkalinity		
P = M	Only OH⁻	M	-	-
P = ½ M	Only CO_3^{2-}	-	2P	-
P = 0	Only	-	-	M
P > ½ M	OH⁻ & CO_3^{2-}	(2P-M)	2(M-P)	-
P < ½ M	CO_3^{2-} & HCO_3^-	-	2P	(M-2P)

Procedure:
Part I
Standardization of HCl solution using standard Na_2CO_3 solution

Pipette out 25-ml std. Na_2CO_3 solution in a 250 ml conical flask. Add 1-2 drops of methyl orange/red indicator to it. The color of solution turns to yellow. Titrate this reaction mixture with HCl solution from the burette till the solution color turns to light pink/orange. This is the end point of titration. Repeat the same procedure to get successive constant end point.

Observation Table

S. No	Volume of Na_2CO_3 solution (V$_1$ ml)	Volume of HCl solution		Constant reading (V$_2$ml)
		Initial Reading	Final Reading	

Calculations:-

Given Normality of Na_2CO_3 solution $= N_1$

Standard Na_2CO_3 solution   HCl solution

N_1 x V_1 N_2 x V_2

$$N_2 = N_1 \text{ x } V_1 / V_2$$

The given normality of HCl solution is = ...

Part II

Estimation of type and extent of alkalinity present in sample A

Pipette out 25-ml water sample A in a 250 ml conical flask. Add 1-2 drops of phenolphthalein as an indicator. The solution becomes pink. Titrate this solution with acid solution from the burette. At the end point the pink color of the solution changes to colorless. Note this end point as P point. Now At this point, add 2 drops of methyl orange indicator to the same solution. Solution becomes yellow. Continue the titration without refilling the burette the solution till the color of solution turns to orange / pink. Note this end point as M point of the titration. Repeat the same procedure to get successive constant readings of P and M point.

The relationship between P point and M point denotes the type and extent of alkalinity present in the given water samples as shown in earlier table1

Observation table

Given water sample A Vs HCl solution
Control reading:
P point: ....ml
M Point: : .... ml

S. No	Vol of given water sample A(V_2 ml)	Volume of HCl solution (ml)			End point (ml) P = M =
		Initial reading	P point	M point	

For sample A P = ...ml and M = ...ml
If P > ½ M
Then
The types of alkalinity present in given water sample A is OH⁻ & CO_3^{2-}
So that

Volume of acid corresponding to OH⁻ = 2P-M &

Volume of acid corresponding to CO_3^{2-} = 2(M-P)

(i) Normality of water sample due to OH⁻

$$\begin{array}{lcl} \text{HCl} & & \text{Water sample A} \\ N_2V_2 & = & N_3V_3 \\ N_2 \times 2P\text{-}M & = & N_3V_3 \end{array}$$

$$N_2 \times 2P\text{-}M \ / 25 \ = \ N_3$$

$$\ldots\ldots\ldots\ldots\ldots \ = \ N_3$$

Weight per litre for OH⁻ $= N_3 \times$ Eqv. weight of $CaCO_3$
$= N_3 \times 50$
$= \ldots\ldots\ldots\ldots.g/l$
$= \ldots\ldots\ldots\ldots.g/l \times 1000 \ mg/l$
$= \ldots\ldots\ldots\ldots.ppm$

(ii)Normality of water sample due to CO_3^{2-}

HCl		Water sample A
N_2V_2	$=$	N_4V_4
$N_2 \times 2 \ (M\text{-}P)$	$=$	N_4V_4
$N_2 \times 2P\text{-}M \ /25$	$=$	N_4
$\ldots\ldots\ldots\ldots\ldots$	$=$	N_4

Weight per litre for OH⁻ $= N_4 \times$ Eqv. weight of $CaCO_3$
$= N_4 \times 50$
$= \ldots\ldots\ldots\ldots.g/l$
$= \ldots\ldots\ldots\ldots.g/l \times 1000 \ mg/l$
$= \ldots\ldots\ldots\ldots.ppm$

Results:The given water sample A contains:-

OH⁻ Alkalinity $=\ldots\ldots\ldots\ldots\ldots..ppm \ CaCO_3$ equivalent

CO_3^{2-} Alkalinity $=\ldots\ldots\ldots\ldots\ldots..ppm \ CaCO_3$ equivalent

Total Alkalinity $=\ldots\ldots\ldots\ldots\ldots \ ppm \ CaCO_3$ equivalent

Experiment 2

Estimation of temporary, permanent and total hardness present in supplied hard water sample by complexometric method

Chemicals Required: Standard hard water (sample A), ethylene diamine tetra-acetic acid solution as an Intermediate solution (Sample B), Buffer solution ($NH_4Cl + NH_4OH$ having pH $= 10$), Eriochrome Black-T indicator solution.

Principle: Hard water contains the dissolved salts of calcium, magnesium and iron ions which are called hardening ions. In low concentrations these ions are not considered harmful for domestic use, but at higher concentrations of these ions interfere with the cleansing action of soaps and accelerate the corrosion of steel pipes, especially those carrying hot water.

Hardening ions, such as Ca^{2+} and Mg^{2+}, form insoluble compounds with soaps. Soaps, which are sodium salts of fatty acids such as sodium stearate, $C_{17}H_{35}COONa$, are very effective cleansing agents so long as they remain soluble; the presence of the hardening ions however causes the formation of a gray, insoluble soap scum such as $(C_{17}H35COO)_2Ca$.

$$2C_{17}H_{35}CO_2^-\ Na^+(aq) + Ca^{2+}(aq) \rightarrow (C_{17}H_{35}CO_2)_2Ca(s) + 2Na^+(aq)$$

Groundwater becomes hard as it flows through underground limestone (CaCO3) deposits; generally, the water from deep wells has a higher hardness than that from shallow wells because of a longer contact time with the limestone. Surface water similarly accumulates hardening ions as a result of flowing over limestone deposits. In either case the CO_2 dissolved in rainwater solubilizes limestone deposits.

$$CaCO_3(s) + CO_2(aq) + H_2O(l) \rightarrow Ca^{2+}(aq) + 2HCO_3^-(aq)$$

Hard water is also responsible for the appearance and undesirable formation of "boiler scale". The boiler scale is a poor conductor of heat and thus reduces the efficiency of transferring heat.

Experimental background:

Complexometry involves the interaction of an organic compound with a complexable metal ion and results in the formation of compounds known as Werner's complexes. The organic compound is an anion or a Lewi's base and is known as Ligand. Several factors, such as pH, basicity of ligand, type of ring formed etc. govern the successful formation of a complex. Thus

$$X L \quad + M^{n+} \quad \text{---------} \rightarrow \quad (L)_x M$$

Ligand   Metal ion   Complex

In this experiment a titration technique is used to measure the combined Ca^{2+} and Mg^{2+} concentrations in a water sample. The titrant or the intermediate solution is the disodium salt of ethylene diamine tetraacetic acid (abbreviated Na2H2Y or EDTA). Its structure is as below

NaOOC-H₂C   CH₂-COOH

\   /

N-CH₂-CH₂-N

/   \

HOOC-H₂C   CH₂COONa

Disodium salt of EDTA

In aqueous solution Na_2H_2Y dissociates into Na^+ and H_2Y^{-2} ions. The H_2Y^{-2}ion reacts with the hardening ions, $Ca^{2+}$and Mg^{2+}, to form very stable complex ions, especially in a solution buffered at a pH of about 10. As Ca^{2+} and Mg^{2+} is present in the hard water and EDTA solution are adding from the burette, it complexes with the "free" Ca^{2+} and Mg^{2+} of the water sample to form the respective complex ions:

$$Ca^{2+}(aq) + H2Y^{2-}(aq) \rightarrow CaY^{2-}(aq) + 2H^+(aq)$$

$$Mg^{2+}(aq) + H2Y^{2-}(aq) \rightarrow MgY^{2-}(aq) + 2H^+(aq)$$

From the balanced equations, once the molar concentration of the Na_2H_2Y solution is known, the moles of hardening ions in a water sample can be calculated from a 1:1 stoichiometric ratio. Thus it is evident that 1 mole of the complex forming H_2Y^{2-}reacts in with one mole of the metal ion and, two moles of hydrogen ions are generated. It is apparent from the equation above that the dissociation of the complex will be governed by the pH of the solution. Lowering of the pH will decrease the stability of the metal EDTA complex. Thus, pH should be maintained constant by the addition of basic buffer in the reaction mixture.

The structure of EDTA-metal complex is as follows:

An indicator is used to detect the endpoint in the titration, Eriochrome Black T (EBT). Eriochrome black-T is sodium 1 – (1-hydroxy, 2-napthyl azo) 6-nitro – 2 napthol-4, sulphonate.

Hence EBT for the simplicity is represented asNaH$_2$D which gives H2D –ion which exhibits different colours at different pH values

$$H_2D^- \quad \text{-----------}\rightarrow H D^{2-} \quad \text{-------------}\rightarrow \quad D^{3-}$$

pH 6.3	pH 10	pH 11.5
(Red)	(Blue)	(Yellowish Orange)

In the pH range 8-10, the blue form of the indicator HD^{2-} gives a wine red complex with Metal ion.

For Example

$$Mg^{2+} + HD^{2-} \text{ ----------} \rightarrow Mg\ D^{-} + H^{+}$$

Blue   Wine red

It forms complex ions with Ca^{2+} and Mg^{2+} ions, but binds more strongly to Mg^{2+} ions. In this estimation, thus four types of complexes are possible viz :

a) **EBT-----Mg^{2+} complex (Wine red)**

b) **EBT-----Ca^{2+} complex (Wine red**

c) **EDTA -----Mg^{2+} complex (Colourless)**

d) **EDTA-----Ca^{2+} complex (Colourless)**

Their order of stability and consequently, their preference of formation are:

EDTA-----Ca^{2+} > EDTA -----Mg^{2+} > EBT-----Mg^{2+} > EBT-----Ca^{2+}

Because only a small amount of EBT is added, only a small quantity of Mg^{2+} is complexed; no Ca^{2+} ion complexes to EBT-therefore, most of the hardening ions remain "free" in solution. The EBT indicator is sky-blue in solution but forms a wine-red complex ion, $[Mg\text{-}EBT]^{2+}$

$$pH$$

$$EBT + Mg^{2+} \text{--------} \rightarrow EBT\text{-}Mg^{2+} \text{ Complex}$$

$$8\text{-}10 \qquad \qquad \text{(Wine red colour obtained)}$$

Before any EDTA solution is added for the analysis, the reaction mixture is wine-red because of the [Mg-EBT] $^{2+}$ complex ion. Once the EDTA complexes all of the "free" Ca^{2+} and Mg^{2+} from the water sample, it then removes the trace amount of Mg^{2+} from the wine-red [Mg-EBT] $^{2+}$ complex ion. The solution changes from wine-red back to the sky-blue color of the EBT indicator, and the endpoint is reached- all of the hardening ions have been complexed with EDTA. The reaction is given as follows:

$$pH$$

$$EDTA + Ca^{2+} \text{--------} \rightarrow EDTA\text{-}Ca^{2+} \text{ complex (Colourless)}$$

$$8\text{-}10$$

$$pH$$

$$EDTA + Mg^{2+} \text{--------} \rightarrow EDTA\text{-} Mg^{2+} \text{ complex (Colourless)}$$

$$8\text{-}10$$

$$\text{EDTA} + \text{EBT-Mg}^{2+} \text{ complex} \xrightarrow[\text{8-10}]{\text{pH}} \text{EDTA-Mg}^{2+} \text{ complex} + \text{EBT}$$

(Wine red)   (blue)

PROCEDURE

Part A: Standardization of EDTA solution using standard hard water sample

Pipette out 25 ml. of standard hard watersolution in a clean conical flask. To it add 5 ml buffer solution ($NH_4Cl + NH_4OH$) and 3-4 drops of internal indicator EBT. The whole solution becomes wine-red in colour. Titrate this solution against EDTA solution from the burette. A change of colour of the solution from wine-red to blue indicates end point. Repeat the same procedure to get successive constant reading.

Part B: Estimation of total hardness present in given water sample C

Pipette out 25 ml. of the hard water sample C into a 250 ml. conical flask. To it add 5 ml buffer solution ($NH_4Cl + NH_4OH$) and 3-4 drops of internal indicator EBT. The whole solution becomes wine-red in colour. Titrate this solution against EDTA solution from the burette. A change of colour of the solution from wine-red to blue indicates end point. Repeat the same procedure to get successive constant reading

Part C: Estimation of Parmanant hardness present in given water sample C

Pipette out 100 ml of given hard water sample C in 250 ml borosil conical flask. Boil this solution gently to reduce to 1/3rdof its original volume. Filter this warmed solution into 250 ml volumetric flask. After complete transfer of boiled sample, remove the filter paper. Wash the funnel properly with distilled water and collect the washings in the volumetric flask. Then make up the volume up to the mark of volumetric flask using distilled water. Shake the solution and then transfer it to 250 ml clean beaker.

Now pipette out 25 ml of diluted hard water sample C and add 5 ml buffer solution ($NH_4Cl + NH_4OH$) and 3-4 drops of internal indicator EBT to it. Titrate this reaction mixture with EDTA solution from the burrete until the wine red colour changes into blue. Repeat the same procedure to get successive constant reading.

Observation Table:

Part 1: Standardization of EDTA solution using standard hard water sample

Standard Hard Water Sample Vs EDTA solution

S. No	Volume of standard Hard Water (V_1 ml)	Volume of EDTA solution		Constant reading (V_2ml)
		Initial Reading	Final Reading	

Part 2: Estimation of Total Hardness present in given water sample C.

Water Sample C Vs EDTA solution

S. No	Volume of given Hard Water sample	Volume of EDTA solution	Volume of EDTA

	C (V_3 ml)			used
		Initial Reading	Final Reading	

Part C: Estimation of Parmanant hardness present in given water sample C

Diluted Water Sample C Vs EDTA solution

S. No	Volume of diluted Hard Water sample C(V_3 ml)	Volume of EDTA solution		Volume of EDTA used
		Initial Reading	Final Reading	

Calculations:

For part 1: Standardization of EDTA solution using standard hard water sample

Let W g of hardness causing salt is dissolved in Y ml of water.

Normality of standard Hard Water

$$= (W \times 1000) / (\text{Eqv weight of salt} \times Y)$$
$$= N_1$$

Std Hard Water = EDTA Solution

$$N_1 \times V_1 = N_2 \times V_2$$

$$N_1 \times V_1 / V_2 = N_2$$

.... Normality of EDTA

Part 2: Determination of total hardness present in given water sample

EDTA= Water sample

$$N_2 \times V_2 = N_3 \times V_3$$

$$N_2 \times V_2 / V_3 = N_3$$

.... Normality of Hard Water

Therefore the amount of total hardness present in given water sample can be calculated as

Weight/litre = N_3 x Eqv weight of $CaCO_3$ x 1000

=A mg/litre $CaCO_3$Equivalent hardness

Part C: Estimation of Permanent hardness present in given water sample C

Diluted water sample C = EDTA Solution

$$N_2 \times V_2 = N_3 \times V_3$$

$$N_3 \times V_3 / V_2 = N_2$$

.... Normality of diluted hard water

So the permanent hardness can be calculated as

Weight per litre = N_2 x Eqv weight of $CaCO_3$ x 1000

$$= B \text{ mg/litre } CaCO_3 \text{Equivalent hardness}$$

This much amount of hardness is present in diluted water sample C But, 250 ml diluted water sample C is prepared from 100 ml water sample C i.e. 2.5 times diluted.Hence, permanent hardness in water sample C = B x 2.5 mg/ lit $CaCO_3$ equivalent hardness.Therefore, Temporary hardness present in given water sample C

= (A-B) mg/ lit $CaCO_3$ equivalent hardness

Result:

The amount of hardness present in given sample C is as follows:

Permanent Hardness = mg/ lit CaCO3 equivalent hardness

Temporary Hardness = mg/ lit CaCO3 equivalent hardness

Total Hardness = mg/ lit CaCO3 equivalent hardness

Experiment 3

Determine the percentage composition of sodium hydroxide in the given mixture of sodium hydroxide and sodium chloride

Apparatus Requirements: Burette, pipette, conical flasks, beakers,

Chemical Requirement: 0.1 N HCl Sodium Hydroxide, Sodium chloride Phenolphthalein Indicator.

Principle

For the titration of a solution of NaOH and NaCl the other solution need is HCl solution. NaOH react with HCl solution whereas NaCl will remain as such.

$$NaOH + HCl \rightarrow NaCl + H2O$$

The mixture solution will be titrated with the acid solution of HCl and we can find out the normality and strength of NaOH. By dividing the strength of NaOH from the total known strength of the solution we will find out the strength of NaCl and hence find the % composition

Indicator: Phenolphthalein, End point - Pink to colorless.

Procedure:

1. Rinse the burette with the given N/10 HCl solution.

2. Take the HCl in the burette and note the initial reading.

3. Pipette out the 10 ml of the solution in the conical flask

4. Add a drop of indicator in the solution
5. Add the acid solution from burette in to the conical flask till solution become colourless

6. Note the burette reading

7. Repeat the experiment to get three concordant reading

Observations:

Normality of the HCl solution = 0.1 N

Volume of the mixture of the in conical flask= 10 ml

S. No	Volume of NaOH solution	Volume of HCl solution		Volume of 0.1 HCl used
		Initial Reading	Final Reading	

Calculations:

By the law of chemical equivalents $N_1V_1 = N_2V_2$

Normality of given NaOH solution $N_2 = N_1V_1 / V_2 = 0.1 \times V_1 / 10$

$= V_1 / 100$

As the equivalent weight of NaOH = 40

Strength of given NaOH solution $= N_2 \times 40$ gm/l $= y$..... g/l

Because the amount of NaOH in the mixture is y g/L

Amount of NaCl in the mixture $= (8 - y)$ g/L $= z$ .. g/L

The percentage of the NaOH $= y/8 \times 100$,

The percentage of NaCl $= z/8 \times 100$

Result: i) Normality of Sodium Hydroxide solution =...................N.
ii) Strength of Sodium Hydroxide solution = ...gm/l.
iii) The percentage of the NaOH = ...y/8 x 100,
iv)The percentage 0f NaCl =........................... z/8 x 100

Experiment 4

Determine the amount of Oxalic acid and Sulphuric acid in one litre of solution, given standard sodium hydroxide and Potassium Permanganate

Apparatus Required: Burette, pipette, conical flasks, beakers, hot plate,

Chemical Required: Solution of oxalic acid and sulphuric acid, Sodium Hydroxide (0.1 N), $KMnO_4$ solution (0.1 N), Phenolphthalein Indicator.

Principle: This experiment involves double titration.

IstTitration: NaOH reacts with oxalic acid as well as H2SO4 according to the following equation

$$2NaOH \quad + \quad (COOH)_2.2H_2O \quad \longrightarrow \quad (COONa)_2 + 4\,H_2O$$

Sodium hydroxide   Oxalic Acid   Sodium oxalate   Water

$$H_2SO_4 + 2NaOH \quad \longrightarrow \quad Na_2SO_4 + 2H_2O$$

By titrating NaOH against the given mixture of oxalic acid and sulphuric acid, the total normality of oxalic acid and sulphuric acid can be determined.

IIndTitration:

The mixture of solution is titrated with N/10 $KMnO_4$ which will react with oxalic acid in the presence of H_2SO_4.

$$2KMnO_4 + 3H_2SO_4 \quad \longrightarrow \quad K_2SO_4 + 2MnSO_4 + 3H_2O + 5(O)$$

$$(COOH)_2 + (O) \quad \underrightarrow{60\text{-}70^\circ C} \quad 2CO_2 + H_2O$$

$$2KMnO_4 + 3H_2SO_4 + 5H_2C_2O_4 \quad \longrightarrow \quad K_2SO_4 + 2MnSO_4 + 8H_2O + 10CO_2$$

So the normality of oxalic acid can be find out by IInd titration and hence its strength is determined. From the normality of the solution obtained in the Ist titration, the normality of oxalic acid is subtracted and hence the normality of H_2SO_4 and its strength can be found out.

Procedure:

Ist Titration:

i) Take 0.1 N NaOH solution in the washed and rinsed burette and pipette out 10 ml of mixture in the titration flask.

ii) Add a drop of phenolphthalein and titrate it till the end point.

iii) Note down the volume of NaOH used.

iv) Repeat the process to get 3 concordant readings.

IInd Titration:

i) Wash and rinse the apparatus thoroughly. Take 0.1 N KMnO$_4$ solution in burette. Since it is a coloured solution we note the upper meniscus for taking the initial and subsequent readings.

ii) Pipette out 10ml. of the mixture in the titration flask. Add almost 10 ml of sulphuric acid and then heat till titration flask is unbearable to 60-70°C.

iii) Titrate till end point and note the volume of KMnO$_4$ used.

iv) Repeat the process to get 3 concordant readings.

Observations:

Table 1: Titration between NaOH and mixture solution

S.No	Volume of	Burette Reading	Volume of

	sample solution taken (ml)			standard NaOH solution used (ml)
		Initial	Final	

Table 2: Titration between $KMnO_4$ and mixture solution

S.No	Volume of sample solution taken (ml)	Burette Reading		Volume of standard NaOH solution used (ml)
		Initial	Final	

Calculations:

From Titration – I

$\qquad N_1V_1$ (H_2SO_4+ Oxalic Acid) = N_2V_2(NaOH)

$\qquad N_1 = 0.1$ x V_2/ 20

From Titration – II

$\qquad N_3V_3$ (Oxalic Acid) = N_4V_4($KMnO4$)

$\qquad N_3 = 0.1$ x V_2/ 20

Where,

Normality of (H_2SO_4+ Oxalic Acid) = N_1

Normality of Oxalic Acid) = N_3

Normality of H_2SO_4 $= N_1 - N_3$

Strength of oxalic acid $= N_3$ x Eq. Wt. of oxalic acid

Strength of H_2SO_4 $= (N_1 - N_3)$ x Eq. Wt. of Sulphuric acid

Result:

i) The strength of oxalic acid = ...gms/l.

ii) The strength of sulphuric acid = ...gms/l.

Experiment 5

Determination of Chloride by the Mohr Method

Introduction

Chloride in the form of chloride (Cl^-) ion is one of the major inorganic anions in water and wastewater. The chloride concentration is higher in wastewater than in raw water because sodium chloride is a common article of diet and passes unchanged through the digestive system(Average estimate of excretion: 6 g of chlorides/person/day; additional chloride burden due to human consumption on wastewater: 15 mg/L). Along the sea coast chloride may be present in high concentration because of leakage of salt water into the sewage system. It also may be increased by industrial process. In potable water, the salty taste produced by chloride concentration is variable and depends on the chemical composition of water. Some waters containing 250 mg/L Cl^- may have a detectable salty taste if sodium cationis present. On the other hand, the typical salty taste may be absent in waters containing as much as 1000 mg/L when the predominant cations are calcium and magnesium. In addition, a high chloride contents may harm metallic pipes and structures as well as growing plants. The measured chloride ions can be used to know salinity of different water sources. For brackish water (or sea water or industrial brine solution), it is an important parameter and indicates the extent of desalting of apparatus required. It also interferes with COD determination and thus it requires a correction to be made on thebasis of amount present or else a complexing agent, such as

$HgSO4$ can be added. Further, chloride ions are used as tracer ions in column studies to model fate of different contaminants in soil and liquid media.

Titrimetric methods based upon silver nitrate are sometimes termed argentometric methods. Potassium chromate can serve as an end point indicator for the argentometric determination of chloride, bromide and cyanide ions by reacting with silver ions to form a brick-red silver chromate precipitate in the equivalence point region.

The Mohr method uses chromate ions as an indicator in the titration of chloride ions with a silver nitrate standard solution. After all the chloride has been precipitated as white silver chloride, the first excess of titrant results in the formation of a silver chromate precipitate, which signals the end point(1).

The reactions are:

$$Ag^+ + Cl^- \leftrightarrow AgCl(s)$$

$$2Ag^+ + CrO_4^{2-} \leftrightarrow Ag_2CrO_4(s)$$

By knowing the stoichiometry and moles consumed at the end point, the amount of chloride in unknown sample can be determined.

Materials

The solid reagents unsed in this experiments were $NaCl$, $CaCO_3$, $NaHCO_3$, K_2CrO_4 and $AgNO_3$.

Methods

Preparation of 5% K_2CrO_4 (indicator):1.0g of K_2CrO_4 was dissolved in 20mL of distilled water

Preparation of standard $AgNO_3$ solution: 9.0 g of$AgNO_3$ was weighed out, transferred to a 500 mL volumetric flsk and made up to volume with distilled water.

The resulting solution was approximately 0.1M.This solution was standardized against NaCl.

Reagent-grade NaCl was dried overnight and cooled to room temperature.0.2500 g portions of NaCl were weighed into Erlenmeyer flasks and dissolved in about 100mLof distilled water. In order to adjust the pH of the solutions, small quantities of $NaHCO_3$ were added until effervescence ceased.About2mLof K_2CrO_4 was added and the solution was titrated to the first permanent appearance of red Ag_2CrO_4

Determination of Cl⁻ in solid sample

The unknown was dried at110 ^0C for1hour and cooled in a desiccator. Individual samples were weighed into 250-mLErlenmeyer flasks and dissolved in about 100 mL of distilled water. Small quantities of $NaHCO_3$ were added until effervescence ceased. About 2mL of K_2CrO_4 was introduced and the solution was titrated to the first permanent appearance of red Ag_2CrO_4 .An indicator blank was determined by suspending a small amount of chloride free $CaCO_3$ in100 mL of distilled water containing 2mLof K_2CrO_7 .

Standardization of $AgNO_3$			
S No	Sample, g NaCl	Vol. of AgNO₃ used(ml)	Conc. of AgNO₃,(M)
Blank	-	0.20	-
1	0.2500	42.90	0.1002
2	0.2750	47.20	0.1001
3	0.2500	42.80	0.1004

Calculation

mmoles of $AgNO_3$ = 0.2500g NaCl/ 58.44 g mol^{-1} x 1000 m mol NaCl

$$= 4.278 \text{ mmols}$$

Molarity of $AgNO_3$ = 4.278/ (42.9 – 0.2) = 1.002 M

Molarity of $AgNO_3$ = (0.1002 +0.1001 + 0.1004) / 3 = 0.1002 M

Determination of Chloride in unknown		
S No	Wt of unknown , g	Vol. of AgNO$_3$ used(ml)	% (w/w) Cl$^-$ in unknown
1	0.2000	26.90	47.4
2	0.2500	33.70	47.6
3	0.1800	24.30	47.6

Mmoles of Cl$^-$ = M $_{AgNO3}$ x V $_{AgNO3}$ = 0.1002 x (26.90 – 0.20) = 2.675

Mass of Cl$^-$ =2.675 x 35.45 =94.83 mg

% Cl$^-$ =94.83 / 200 mg sample x 100 = 47.4 %

% Cl$^-$ in unknown = 47.5 ± 0.1

Experiment 6

To determine Chemical Oxygen Demand (COD) of a given water sample.

Apparatus:

Reflux apparatus, consisting of a 250 ml.-flat bottomed Borosil flask with ground glass joint and a condenser.

Regents required:

1. Standard 0.25 N $K_2Cr_2O_7$ solution

2. Sulfuric acid-silver sulphate reagent:

3. Standard 0.1 N Fe $(NH_4)_2SO_4.7H_2O$ solution:

4. Ferroin indicator

5. $HgSO_4$

Figure: Structure of ferroin indicator

Theory: In Environmental Chemistry, the Chemical Oxygen Demand (COD) test is commonly used to measure the amount of organic compounds that is susceptible to oxidation by a strong oxidant present in water. Any organic matter such as hydrocarons when brought in contact with oxygen is oxidised to get CO_2 and H_2O. If the organic matter contains hydrogen, nitrogen, sulphur, etc. in addition to carbon, then the chemical oxidation leads to formation of CO_2, H_2O, NO_2, SO_2 and etc. To get this oxidation, oxygen is required and demanded by this organic material. The possibility of meeting such demand is through dissolved oxygen in the water. Thus dissolved oxygen in water gets depleted and survival of the bio-organisms in such water is difficult and sometimes impossible. It is therefore, essential to check COD of effluent water before letting it out from industry. It is expressed in milligrams per liter (mg/L), which indicates the mass of oxygen consumed per liter of solution. Older references may express the units as parts per million (ppm).

The basis for the COD test is that nearly all organic compounds can be fully oxidized to carbon dioxide with a strong oxidizing agent under acidic conditions. The amount of oxygen required to oxidize an organic compound to carbon dioxide, ammonia, and water is given by:

$$C_n H_a O_b N_c + \left(n + \frac{a}{4} - \frac{b}{2} - \frac{3}{4}c\right) O_2 \rightarrow nCO_2 + \left(\frac{a}{2} - \frac{3}{2}c\right) H_2O + cNH_3$$

This expression does not include the oxygen demand caused by the oxidation of ammonia into nitrate. The process of ammonia being converted into nitrate is referred to as nitrification. The following is the correct equation for the oxidation of ammonia into nitrate.

$$NH_3 + 2O_2 \rightarrow NO_3^- + H_3O^+$$

The second equation should be applied after the first one to include oxidation due to nitrification if the oxygen demand from nitrification must be known. Dichromate does not oxidize ammonia into nitrate, so this nitrification can be safely ignored in the standard chemical oxygen demand test.

Using potassium dichromate

Potassium dichromate is a strong oxidizing agent under acidic conditions. (Acidity is usually achieved by the addition of sulfuric acid.) The reaction of potassium dichromate with organic compounds is given by:

$$C_nH_aO_bN_c + dCr_2O_7^{2-} + (8d + c)H^+ \rightarrow nCO_2 + \frac{a + 8d - 3c}{2}H_2O + cNH_4^+ + 2dCr^{3+}$$

where d = 2n/3 + a/6 - b/3 - c/2.

Most commonly, a 0.25 N solution of potassium dichromate is used for COD determination, although for samples with COD below 50 mg/L, a lower concentration of potassium dichromate is preferred.In the process of oxidizing the organic substances found in the water sample, potassium dichromate is reduced (since in all redox reactions, one reagent is oxidized and the other is reduced), forming Cr3+. The amount of Cr3+is determined after oxidization is complete, and is used as an indirect measure of the organic contents of the water sample.

Importance of Blank Titration

Because COD measures the oxygen demand of organic compounds in a sample of water, it is important that no outside organic material be accidentally added to the sample to be measured. To control for this, a so-called blank sample is required in the determination of COD (and BOD, for that matter). A blank sample is created by adding all reagents (e.g. acid and oxidizing agent) to a volume of distilled water. COD is measured for both the water and blank samples, and the two are compared. The oxygen demand in the blank sample is subtracted from the COD for the original sample to ensure a true measurement of organic matter.

Interference due to Chlorides in waste water

Some samples of water contain high levels of oxidizable inorganic materials which may interfere with the determination of COD. Because of its high concentration in most wastewater, chloride is often the most serious source of interference. Its reaction with potassium dichromate follows the equation:

$$6Cl^- + Cr_2O_7^{2-} + 14H^+ \rightarrow 3Cl_2 + 2Cr^{3+} + 7H_2O$$

Prior to the addition of other reagents, mercuric sulfate can be added to the sample to eliminate chloride interference.

Procedure:

Part –I Determination of COD value of the given waste water sample

Pipette out 10 ml of the wastewater sample in a reflux flask, dilute the sample by 20 ml with distilled water. Mix well and add 10 ml.of 0.25 N K2Cr2O7 solutions. Drop some pumice stones and slowly add 30 ml. of H2SO4—AgSO4 reagent while continuously swirling the flask. If the colour changes to green, add more K2Cr2O7 and or alternatively discard the solution and take a fresh sample with lesser aliquot. Mix the contents of the flask thoroughly. Connect the flask to the condenser and slowly heat flask. Reflux for at least 2 hours. Cool and wash down the condenser with distilled water such that the washings fall in to the flask. Add few drops of Ferroin indicator and titrate the content of the flask (unreacted K2Cr2O7) with the 0.1 N FAS solution. Near the end point the yellow colour of the solution gradually fades up to bluish green, continue the titration till bluish green colour changes to wine red color.

Part-II Blank Titration

Repeat the above procedure using 10 ml of the distilled water instead of the Waste water sample for about half hour.

Part-III Standardization of the FAS solution

Pipette out 10 ml of the $K_2Cr_2O_7$ solution in a conical flask add few drops of the Ferroin indicator and titrate with the standard FAS solution till solution changes color from yellow to wine red colour.

Calculation

Part A Standardization of FAS solution

$$K_2Cr_2O_7 \text{ solution } = \text{ FAS Solution}$$
$$N_1V_1 \qquad = N_2V_2$$
$$N_2 \qquad = N_1V_1 / V_2$$

Part B: Determination of COD of given water sample

COD (mg/l) $\qquad = (V_4-V_3) \times N_2 \times 8 \times 1000 / V$

Where,

V_4 = Volume of the FAS run down in the blank experiment
V_3 = Volume of the FAS run down in the testexperiment
N_2 = Normality of FAS solution
V = Volume of the test sample taken

Result: The Chemical oxygen demand of the given waste water sample was found to be equal to _____ppm.

Experiment 7

Determination of Calorific Value of fuel by Bomb Calorimeter.

To determine the calorific value of a solid fuel, using Bomb Calorimeter

THEORY

The calorific value is the most important property of a fuel. The calorific value may be defined as the total quantity at heat, liberated by the complete combustion of a unit mass of the fuel. The calorific value determines the quantity of a fuel, and also helps in calculating thermal fuel, and a thermal efficiency and heat balan ce in the process where coal is used as a fuel.

HIGH OR GROSS CALORIFIC VALUE:-The higher or GCV is defined as the total amount of heat liberated when one unit mass of the fuel has been completely burnt & the products of combustion have been cooled to room temperature. In such case water vapour produced by combustion of hydrogen and evaporisation of moisture coil get condensed and the heat is evolved. It is also taken into consideration. However, the heat evolved due to formation of H_2SO_4 and HNO_3during combustion are subtracted from the heat evolved. The calorific value, as determined in the lab by bomb calorimeter represent the GCV.

LOWER OR NET CALORIFIC VALUE:-

In actual practice, the water vapour produced from hydrogen and moisture of the fuel during combustion is not condensed and escapes as such along with the hot combustic gases and hence a lesser amount of heat is available, hence, LCV or net calorific value may be defined as the net heat

LCV = GCV - [Latent heat of water vapour formed]

DISCRIPTION :-The calorific value of a solid or non-volatile liquid fuel is usually determined with the help of an oxygen bomb calorimeter.

The calorific value determination is carried out in a bomb calorimeter which consists of following parts as shown in figure

(i) The combustion bomb(ii) The calorific vessel (iii) The water jacket (iv) Stirrer (v) Thermometer (vi) Crucible (vii) Oxygen (viii) Firing wire

WORKING

A known amount of sample (1gm) is burnt in a sealed chamber called bomb. The air replaced by pure O_2. Heat produced by burning the fuel must be equal to the amount of heat absorbed by the calorimeter before calculating the calorific value of a fuel with the help of bomb calorimeter. The water equivalent of the apparatus must be first determine.

CALCULATION:-X = mass of fuel sample

W = Mass of water

w = Mass of water equivalent

t1= initial temperature of water

t2= Final temperature of water

L = HCV in cal./gm

Heat liberated by fuel – Heat absorbed by water

$XL = (W+w) (t_2 - t_1)$

or $L = \dfrac{(W+w)\ (t_2-t_1)}{X}$ cal/gm

MATERIAL:-Bomb calorimeter, given fuel sample, benzoic acid, burette, pipette, measuring, flask, N/10 NaOH, Analytical balance.

PROCEDURE:-

A known mass (about 0.5 to 1.0 gm) of given fuel is taken in clean & dry crucible. The crucible is then supported over the ring. A fine pt. wire, touching the fuel sample is then stretched across electrodes and cotton piece or thread of known wt. is tied to the pt. wire inserted in the sample inside. The core should be taken so that the lower end of the cotton thread touches the sample. Place 10 ml of distilled water inside the bomb with the help of pipette & place the cover in position and disconnect the O2supply. The bomb is then placed inside the vessel.

PRECAUTIONS:

1. Do not use too much of the sample in any case. (Not more than 1 gm) Since bomb may not withstay for long-long time it effects for combustible change which liberate near than 10,000 calorie.

2. Do not change with more O_2 than necessary O_2 to obtain complete combustion and don't fire the bomb if an average of O2is advice.

Experiment 8

Determination of flash point of a combustible liquid by Able's closed cup flash point apparatus

Theory

The Flash Point of oil may be defined as the minimum temperature to which it must be heated to give off sufficient vapour to ignite momentarily when a flame of standard dimensions is brought near the surface of the sample for a prescribed rate in an apparatus of specified dimensions. This is detected by the appearance of momentary flash upon the application of small flame over the surface of oil. The Flash Point is defined as closed cup or open cup flash point accordingly as the apparatus for the determination of flash point of sample is provided with a cover to cover the sample cup or not.The mechanism of the appearance of the flash can be explained in the following manner. Every flammable liquid has a vapour pressure, which is a function of the liquid's temperature. As the temperature increase, the vapour pressure increases, as the vapour pressure increases, the concentration of evaporated flammable liquid in the air increases. Hence, temperature determines the concentration of its vapour in the air to sustain combustion. The flash point of a flammable liquid is the lowest temperature at which there can be enough flammable vapour to ignite, when an ignition source is applied. Oil containing minute quantities of volatile organic substances is liable to flash below the true flash point of the oil. Although a small flash may be observed in such cases, it should not be confused with the true flash point, since its intensity does not increase with increase in temperature, as occurredwhen the true flash point is reached

Diagram

Importance of flash point from view of lubricants:

Good lubricating oil should not volatilize under the working temperatures. Even if some volatilization takes place, the vapour formed should not form inflammable mixture with air under the condition of lubrication. From this point of view, the flash point of lubricating oil is of vital importance.

Lubricating oil selected for the job should have a flash point which is reasonably above its working temperature. This insures the safety against the fire hazards during the storage, transport and use of the lubricating oil. This test is immense importance for illuminating and lubricating Oils. This helps in detecting the highly volatile constituents of the oils. If they are highly volatile at ordinary temperature, the issuing vapors may cause fire hazards. So to ensure safety, certain minimum temperatures are laid down for fuels and Lubricating Oils below which they should not give off adequate vapors to make them burn.

OUTLINE OF THE METHOD:

The sample is placed in the oil cup of apparatus and heated at a slow uniform rate about 2 0C. A small test is directed into the cup at regular intervals, and the lowest temperature at which application of the test flame causes the vapor to ignite momentary, with a distinct flash inside the cup,

Description of the apparatus:

The Abel's apparatus consists of the following essential parts:

a. SAMPLE CUP: This is a cylindrical vessel with a lid. Within the cup, near the top; there is a sample level mark.

b. COVER:

(A) COVER: The cup is provided with a close fitting cover. The cover is provided with a thermometer socket, to support an oil test lamp, a movable metal bead. The top of the cover has three rectangular holes which are covered or uncovered by moving the slide which has two perforations to allow air to enter the oil up and bring contact between vapors of the oils and flame of the test-lamp when in open position.A metal bead, the dimension (4mm) of which represents the size of test flame, is mounted in the cover. The apparatus is also provided with a stirrer.

HEATING VESSEL: -

The heating vessel consists of copper vessels and placed coaxially, one inside the other. The space between the two vessels is used as a water jacket. When the oil cup is placed into the hole at the top of the vessel, it fits into it and leaves an air gap between itself and outer copper water vessel.

The water can be heated electrically or with a burner or spirit lamp. Thermometer is provided with the apparatus for the measuring the temperature of the oil sample.

PROCEDURE:

Fill the given sample in such a way that the sample level is exactly up to the mark in the cup. Fix the cup in to the apparatus and cover with lid. Insert thermometer in the thermometer holder given in the cup in such a manner that it will not directly touch the lower bottom of the cup and the paddle stirrer inside the cup. Fill the water bath with the cold water. Close the sliding shutter and light the standard flame. Adjust the size of flame (4mm diameter) with respect to the metal bead. Stir the oil using paddle stirrer. Introduce the flame by opening the shutter and check the appearance of the flash. Now heat the apparatus and set the rate of temperature increase at the rate of 1 to 2 ^{0}C per minute. Check the flash point of given sample at the interval of 3 0C rise in the temperature. Discontinue the stirring the sample during the introduction of the test flame. On observing a flash, stop the heating process and allow the temperature to decrease. Check the occurrence of a flash at every 1 0C drop in temperature at which the flash is observed as the flash point of the sample.

Observation Table 1		
S No	Increasing Temperature (°C)	Interference (No flash or flash observed)
Observation Table 2		
S No	Decreasing Temperature (°C)	Interference (No flash or flash observed)

Result: The Flash Point of given Sample oil No. by Able' Flash Point apparatus is found to be ------0C.

Experiment 9

Determination of relative and kinematic viscosities of a given lubricating oil at different temperatures using Redwood Viscometer No. 1 or No. 2.

Apparatus: Redwood viscometer (1 / 2), thermometer, etc.

THEORY AND GENERAL DISCUSSION:

Viscosity is one of the most important properties of a lubricating oil. Viscosity is a measure of the internal resistance to the motion of a fluid and is mainly due to the forces of cohesion between the fluid molecules. The formation of a fluid film of a lubricant between the moving friction surface and the generation of the frictional heat under the particular condition of load, bearing speed and lubricant supply is mainly depends upon the viscosity of the lubricant and to some extent on its oiliness. If the viscosity of the oil is too low, the fluid lubricant film cannot be maintained between the moving surfaces as a result of which excessive wear may take place. On the other hand, if the viscosity of the oil is too high, excessive friction due to the shearing of oil itself would result. Hence in hydrodynamic lubrication, the lubricant should posses the proper viscosity. So, it is of vital importance to have knowledge of the viscosity of the lubricating oil. Viscosity of the fluid may be measured in several ways, one of which is determining time required for a definite amount of the liquid to flow through a capillary. Such method includes the use of Saybolt, Engler and Redwood Viscometers.

Viscosity may be expressed as dynamic (or absolute) viscosity, kinematic viscosity or the viscosity called after the name of the apparatus used for its determination.

DYNAMIC OR ABSOLUTE VISCOSITY:

Dynamic or absolute viscosity (often denoted by 'n') is the tangential force per unit area required to maintain unit velocity gradient between two parallel planes, in the fluid unit distance apart. It can be also be defined as the ratio of shearing stress to the rate of shearing strain.

If F is the force required to keep moving an particle of surface area A in contact with the fluid, separated from stationary surface by a thickness D, and moving with velocity V, then

Shearing stress = Force acting on the surface area A

$$i.e. \ F/A: \ \text{--------------------------}(1)$$

$$\text{Rate of shearing strain} = V/D \ \text{--------------------------}(2)$$

Absolute Viscosity n = Shearing stress/ rate of shearing strain.

$$\frac{F/A}{V/D} = \frac{F \times D}{V \times A} \qquad \text{--------------}(3)$$

The numerical value of 'n' depends upon the unit used in equation (3). In metric system the unit is 'poise' (F = 1 dyne, A = 1 cm. And V = km/sec.). A smaller unit, the centipoises is more often used. Poise is equal in one dyne/second/cm^2 (Dimensions of absolute viscosity are ML -1T-1). Absolute is also referred to as 'coefficient of viscosity'.

KINEMATIC VISCOSITY: -The ratio of absolute viscosity to density for any fluid is known as absolute kinematics viscosity. It is donated by μ and in C.G.S. system, its units are stokes and centistokes (1/100th of stoke) respectively.

$$\mu = \eta / p$$

Where,

μ = Absolute kinematic viscosity

ŋ = absolute dynamic viscosity

ρ = density of fluid.

Dimension of μ are L2T1

Since the rate, at which a fluid will flow through an apparatus increases as the internal friction of the fluid decreases, the rate of flow through an orifice or short tube may be used as a means for measuring viscosity. This is the principle involved in the Redwood viscometer, which is an English standard whereas Saybolt's Viscometer is used in U.S.A. and Engler's Viscometer in Europe. In these commercial Viscometers a fixed volume of the liquid is allowed to flow (in case of Redwood it is 50 ml. at 270C Engler-60 ml. and Saybolt –200 ml.) through a capillary tube of specified dimension under given set of conditions and the time of flow is measured at a particular temperature. The result is usually expressed in terms of the time in seconds taken by oil to flow through the standard orifice of the particular standard apparatus used.

e.g.: Viscosity of oil is 250, Redwood (no. ½) seconds at 270C. This Viscosity so determined is sometimes called as Relative Viscosity.

Absolute and kinematic Viscosities can also be determined from the relative Viscosity (i.e. Redwood values) from the equations:

$$\mu = Ct \quad \text{----------------(5) (for Fluids)}$$

Whose Kinematic Viscosity is more than 10 centistokes

And

$$M = (Ct-\beta)/t \ldots\ldots\ldots\ldots\ldots(6) \text{ (For fluids kinetimacs Viscosities}$$
less than or equals to 10 centistokes)

Where,

μ = Kinetimac viscosity in centistokes

t = time of flow in seconds

C = viscometer constant

ρ = coefficient of kinetic energy which may be determined experimentally oreliminated by choosing long flow-timesTest Viscometer may be calibrated constant C determined by solutions of known Viscosity. The primary standard used is freshly distilled water, whose kinematics viscosity is 1.0008 centistokes.

Other standards usually employed are:-

40% Sucrose solution

μ = 4.390 cs at 25 ^{0}C, ρ = 1.1739

60% Sucrose solution

μ = 33.66 cs at 25 ^{0}C, ρ = 1.28335

For Redwood Viscometer No1

The values of constant are:

Time of flow, t	β	C
40 - 85 sec	190	0.264
85 - 2000 sec	65	0.247

For Redwood viscometer No 2:

The values of constant are: β = 1120, C = 2.720

Redwood Viscometer No 2 is used for very viscous liquids and gives 1/10th of the value of Redwood Viscometer No 1. Replace the ball value in position to seal the ca to prevent overflow of the oil.

PROCEDURE:

1) Level the instrument by leveling screws ensuring that it is horizontal with the help of spirit level.

2) Put the valve rod at its position (i.e. in the concavity at the bottom of the cup) to close the passage of orifice.

3) Keep clean dry Kohlrausch's flask centrally below the jet.

4) The test sample is poured into the oil cup and adjust the level of oil, with that of the pointer. Later indicates the level to which oil is to be filled.

5) Fill up the water bath with water and adjust the level of water with that of the pointer in the oil cup.

6) Cover the oil cup with the lid and insert thermocouple / thermometer of desired range into the oil cup from the thermometer bracket. Care should be taken that it dose not touch the bottom of the cup.

7) Also insert the thermometer into the water bath from the shield.

8) Let the oil in the cup as well as water of the water bath attain the room temperature . Once the temperature of oil and water bath become steady for a period of 2-3 minutes record the temperatures separately. (Quite likely that there may be a difference of 1-20C between the temperature of oil and the temperature of water in the water bath.

9) Lift up the value rod and suspend it from the thermometer bracket and start the stop watch simultaneously.

10) Receiving flask is so located that oil strikes the flared mouth and does not drop directly into the opening, which would cause foaming.

11) When the level of the oil reaches 50 ml. mark in the neck of the flask, stop the stop-watch.

12) At the same time close the passage of the orifice by keeping the valve rod at its original position to prevent any overflow of oil.

13) The time elapsed in seconds is the relative viscosity of oil at room temperature.

14) Switch on the water bath adjust the knob of the regulator in such a way that the temperature of the water bath is a few degree above temperature i.e. 85^0C

15) Again, pour oil into the cup and adjust oil level as described earlier.

16) Stir the contents of the bath and dup regularly.

17) When the temperature of sample has become quite steady at the desired value i.e. at 850C lift the valve rod and suspend it from the thermometer bracket and start the stopwatch simultaneously.

18) When the level of the oil touches the 50 ml. mark on the neck of theflask stop the watch. The time elapsed in seconds in the relativeviscosity of oil at 850C.

19) Now take out some hot water from the water bath and add equalamount of cold water to bring the temperature of the bath slightlyabove that of test temperature i.e. 750C.

20) Pour oil into the cup and adjust oil level as described earlier.

21) Stir the contents of the bath and cup regularly.

22) When the temperature of sample has become quite steady at the desired temperature i.e. 750C find out the relative viscosity of test sample at this temperature as described earlier.

23) Repeat the procedure to find out relative viscosities of oil at 65 ^{0}C, 50 ^{0}C, 45 ^{0}C, respectively.

24) Record all the results in the tabular form.

25) Construct graph co-relation (a) Viscosity and temperature, (b) Log of viscosity and temperature and (c) Kinematic viscosity and temperature. (d) Log of Kinematic viscosity and temperature, (e) Find viscosity index of the given oil.

Observation Table: Redwood viscometer no.:

S.No	Temp. (^{0}C)	Time (sec)	Relative viscosity (η)	Kinematic viscosity (μ)	log(η)	log(μ)
1	Room Temp					
2	85					
3	75					
4	65					
5	55					
6	45					
7	35					
8						

Calculation

Graphs were plotted between

1. Relative viscosity (r η) against the temperature of sample (T)

2. Log of relative viscosity (r η) against the temperature of sample (T)

3. Kinematic viscosity ( ) μ against the temperature of sample (T)

4. Log of kinematic viscosity ( ) μ against the temperature of sample (T)

And determine the slope of the graph 1 from the plot and calculate it using the least square method.

Result:- The rate of change of relative viscosity with respect to temperature was found to be equal to ....

Experiment 10

Determination of flash point of a combustible liquid by Pensky Martan's closed cup flash point apparatus

DESCRIPTION OF THE APPARATUS

A Pensky Martin apparatus consists of the following parts:

SAMPLE CUP: Sample cup is a cylindrical vessel, made of brass with a filling mark grooved inside near the top. It is provided with a lid.

LID: The lid is equipped with the following parts:

i) Stirrer: The stirring device consists of a vertical steel shaft mounted in the center of the cup and carrying two-bladed brass propellers.

ii) Cover: It has four opening, one for thermometer and the rest for the oxygen entry and exposure of vapors to test flame.

iii) Shutter: The lid is equipped with a brass shutter operating on the plane of the upper surface of the cover. The shutter is so shaped and mounted on the lid that when in one position, the holes are completely closed and when in the other, these orifices are completely opened.

iv) The flame exposure device: The lid is equipped with a pilot lamp with such a mechanism that its flame operates simultaneously with the shutter. When the shutter is in the 'open' position, the tip is lowered down in the center of the central orifice.

v) Heater: The cup is heated by means of burner or it is electrically heated. The air bath has cylindrical interior about 4 cm. deep and can be heated by a direct flame or an electric resistance element. The top-plate is also made of metal and mounted with an air gap between it and the air bath.

Diagram

PROCEDURE:

The cup and its accessories are well cleaned and dried before the test is started. Now the cup is filled with the oil to be tested up to the level indicated by the filling mark and covered with the lid. The stirring device, the thermometer and flame exposure device is fixed on the top of the cover. The cup is now set in the apparatus properly and the thermometer inserted. The test flame is lighted and adjusted until it is the size of a bead (4mm in diameter). The apparatus is heated so that the heating rate is maintained, with the help of a rheostat, at 5-6 0C per minute and stirring rate at 1 to 2 rps.

Once the heating started, the test flames is applied after each 2 0C rise of temperature nearer to the sample in the cup by opening the shutter and check the appearance of the flash.On observing a flash, stop the heating process and allow the temperature to decrease. Check the occurrence of a flash at every 1 0C drop in temperature. Record the lowest temperature at which the flash is observed as the flash point of the sample.

Observation Table 1		
S No	Increasing Temperature (°C)	Interference (No flash or flash observed)

Observation Table 2		
S No	Decreasing Temperature (°C)	Interference (No flash or flash observed)

RESULT: The Flash Point of given sample determined by Pensky Marten's Flash Point apparatus is found to be --------------0C.

Experiment 11

Determination of flash point of a combustible liquid by Cleveland's open cup flash point apparatus

DEFINITIONS:

I) Flash Point: The minimum temperature to which it must be heated to give off sufficient vapour to ignite momentarily when a flame of standard dimensions is brought near the surface of the sample for a prescribed rate in an apparatus of specified dimensions.

II) Fire point: It is defined as the minimum temperature at which the oil gives off sufficient vapor which causes it to burn for a period of 5 seconds or more when a test flame is passed over surface of the oil.

DESCRIPTION OF APPARATUS:

The apparatus consists of a test cup made of without any lid and is equipped with a handle. The cup is supported by a metal plate known as heating plate. The cup may be heated by an electric heater mounted below the cup in the apparatus itself. The metal plate has an extension for mounting the test flame and the thermometer support. The test flame is mounted in such a manner as to permit automatic duplication of the sweep of the test flame over the sample cup. The size of the flame can be adjusted with respect to the dimension of metal bead (4 mm).

Diagram

PROCEDURE:

The apparatus is thoroughly cleaned and the thermometer is suspended in such a way so that the bottom of the thermometer bulb just above the bottom of sample cup. The cup is now filled with sample up to the filling mark grooved on the inner side of

the cup taking care that the surface of the sample is free from bubbles and there is no oil above the filling mark. The test flame is adjusted to have a flame diameter of about 4 mm. Now move the test flame over the sample cup and check the appearance of flash over the sample inside the cup.If no flash observed, increase the temperature of the sample taken and take a flame over the cup after every 2 0C increases. On observing a flash, stop the heating process and allow the temperature to decrease. Check the occurrence of a flash at every 1 0C drop in temperature. Record the lowest temperature at which the flash is observed as the flash point of the sample.

Observation Table 1		
S No	Increasing Temperature (ºC)	Interference (No flash or flash observed)

Observation Table 2		
S No	Decreasing Temperature (ºC)	Interference (No flash or flash observed)

Result:

The Flash Point of given sample determined by Cleveland's apparatus is found to be ----0C

Experiment 12

Estimation of Dissolved Oxygen in Water sample – Winkler's Method

Apparatus:-Burette, pipette, conical flask, beaker, measuring flask and droppers.

Chemicals:-$Na_2S_2O_3$(N/100), $MnSO_4$solution, KI, Starch, conc. H_2SO_4.

Theory:-Oxygen itself is not a pollutant in water but its deficiency is an indicator of several types of pollution in water. Dissolved oxygen (DO) is determined by Winkler's method or iodometric titration. The dissolved oxygen in water oxidizes KI and an equivalent amount of iodine is librated. This iodine is titrated against a standard hypo solution. However since dissolved oxygen in water is in molecular state and is not capable of reacting with KI therefore an oxygen carrier such as manganese hydroxide is used. The method involves introducing a conc. solution of $MnSO_4$, NaOH and potassium iodide, azide reagent, in to the water sample. The white precipitate of $Mn(OH)_2$ formed, is oxidized by oxygen in water sample to give a brown precipitate of basic manganic oxide $MnO(OH)_2$. This $MnO(OH)_2$ in acidic medium dissolves and liberates free iodine from the added KI in an equivalent amount of dissolved oxygen in water sample. This librated I_2 is then titrated against $Na_2S_2O_3$using starch as an indicator. The reactions involved are:-

$$MnSO_4 + 2NaOH \longrightarrow Mn(OH)_2 + Na_2SO_4$$

$$Mn(OH)_2 + O_2 \longrightarrow 2MnO(OH)_2$$
$$\text{Basic Manganic oxide}$$

$$MnO(OH)_2 + H_2SO_4 \longrightarrow MnSO_4 + 2H_2O + O$$

$$2KI + H_2SO_4 + O \longrightarrow K_2SO_4 + H_2O + I_2$$

$$2\,Na_2S_2O_3 + I_2 \longrightarrow Na_2S_4O_6 + 2NaI$$
$$\text{Sodium tetrathionate}$$

The nitrites present in water, interfere with the titration as these can also liberate I_2 form KI.

$$2HNO_2 + H_2SO_4 + 2KI \longrightarrow 2NO + K_2SO_4 + 2H_2O + I_2$$

Thus to destroy nitrite, sodium azide is used.

$$2NaN_3 + H_2SO_4 \longrightarrow 2HN_3 + Na_2SO_4$$

$$\text{(Hydrazoic acid)}$$

$$3HNO_2 + HN_3 \longrightarrow 2NO_2 + 2N_2 + 2H_2O$$

Procedure:-

1. A known amount of sample water(say 250ml) is taken in a stoppered bottle avoiding contact with air.

2. Add 0.2ml of $MnSO_4$solution it by means of a pipette, dipping the end well below the surface of water. Also add 2ml of alkaline iodide – azide solution to it.

3. Stopper the bottle and shake thoroughly. Allow the brown precipitate of $MnO(OH)_2$ formed, to settle down.

4. When some portion of the liquid below the stopper is clear, add 2ml of conc. $H_2SO_4$with the help of pipette. Stopper and mix till the

precipitate is completely dissolved. The characteristics brown colour of iodine is produced.

5. Transfer 100ml of above solution in a 250ml flask with a pipette. Titrate the liberated I2with standardized sodium thiosulphate solution until the sample solution becomes pale yellow.

6. Add 2ml of starch solution the solution will turn blue.

7. Continue titration till the blue colour disappears.

8.Repeat to get another reading.

Precautions:-1. The water should be taken in a stoppered bottle very carefully without trapping air bubbles, which could raise oxygen level by aerating the sample.

2. $MnSO_4$ and alkaline iodine – azide solutions are added to the water sample just below the surface of water.

3. Whole of the precipitate of $MnO(OH)_2$should be dissolved in H_2SO_4

Observations:-Normality of $Na_2S_2O_3$ = N2= N/100

Volume of the water sample taken for titration = V1= 25.0ml

Table:Titration of water sample containing dissolves $O_2$with N/100 $Na_2S_2O_3$ or hypo solution

S.No	Volume of solution taken in titration flask (ml)	Burette reading		Volume of $Na_2S_2O_3$ used (ml)
		Initial	Final	
1				
2				
3				

Calculations

$N_1V_1 = N_2V_2$

N1 = Normality of DO in water sample = ?

V_1 = Volume of water sample containing dissolved oxygen = 25.0ml

N_2 = Normality of $Na_2S_2O_3$ = N/100

V_2 = Volume of $Na_2S_2O_3$ = -------ml

$N_1 = N_2V_2/V_1 = 1/100 \times V_2/25$

Dissolved Oxygen in water sample in g/l = $N_1 \times 8$ g/l

Dissolved Oxygen in water sample in ppm = $N_1 \times 8 \times 10^3$ ppm

Result:-The amount of dissolved oxygen in water = ---------ppm

Experiment 13

Estimation of Iron (II) in an iron tablet by using a standard solution of potassium manganate (VII)

THEORY

To estimate the iron(II) content of an iron tablet, a small number of tablets are first dissolved in dilute sulfuric acid. This solution is then titrated against previously standardised potassium manganate(VII) solution. The reaction is represented by the equation:

$$MnO_4^- + 8H^+ + 5Fe^{+2} \rightarrow Mn^{+2} + 5Fe^{+3} + 4H_2O$$

METHOD

Preparation of tablets: Find the mass of five iron tablets. Crush the weighed tablets in a mortar and pestle. Transfer all the ground material to a beaker where it is dissolved in about 100 cm^3 of dilute sulfuric acid. All of this solution (including washings) is transferred to a 250 cm3 volumetric flask and the solution made up to the mark with deionised water. The volumetric flask should be stoppered and inverted several times. This is the solution containing iron(II) ions. Titration: Wash the pipette, burette and conical flask with deionised water. Rinse the burette with the potassium manganate(VII) solution and the pipette with the iron(II) solution. Using a pipette filler, fill the pipette with the iron(II) solution and transfer the contents of the pipette to the conical flask. Acidify this solution by adding about 10 cm3 of dilute sulfuric acid. Using a funnel, fill the burette with potassium manganate(VII) solution, making sure that the part below the tap is filled before adjusting to zero. Because of the intense colour of KMnO$_4$ solution, readings are taken

Page

from the top of the meniscus. With the conical flask standing on a white tile, add the solution from the burette to the flask. Swirl the flask continuously and occasionally wash down the walls of the flask with deionised water using a wash bottle. The end-point of the titration is detected by 'the first persisting pink colour'. Note the burette reading. Repeat the procedure two or three times, adding the potassium manganate(VII) dropwise approaching the endpoint. These accurate titres should agree to within 0.1 cm3. Calculate the concentration of the iron(II) solution, and from this calculate the mass of iron in an iron tablet.

Specimen results

Mass of iron tablets = 1.81 g   First titre = 17.0 cm^3

Second titre = 16.7 cm^3 Third titre = 16.7 cm^3

Average of accurate titres = 16.7 cm^3

Volume of iron(II) solution used in each titration = 25.0 cm^3

Concentration of potassium manganate(VII) solution = 0.005 M

Calculations

$$V_A \times M_A \times n_B = V_B \times M_B \times n_A$$

$$25.0 \times M_A \times 1 = 16.7 \times 0.005 \times 5 \, M_A$$

$$= 16.7 \times 0.005 \times 5 / (25.0 \times 1)$$

$$= 0.0167 \, M$$

Volume of Fe^{2+} solution in total = 250.0 cm^3

Moles of iron in this volume = 0.0167 = 0.004175

Mass of iron in this volume = 0.004175 x 56 g

$$= 0.2338 \, g$$

Percentage of iron in the tablets = 12.92%

Mass of iron in each tablet = 0.2338 / 5 = 46.76 mg.

Experiment 14

To estimate saponification value of a given oil sample

Introduction

The saponification value of oil is the number of milligrams of potassium hydroxide required to saponify one gram of the oil or fat under the specified conditions.The vegetables or animal oils are esters of fatty acids and glycerol. They react with KOH to form the potassium salts of fatty acids. The saponification value of oil is determined by refluxing a known quantity of the sample with a known excess of standard KOH solution and determining the alkali consumed by titrating the unreacted alkali. It is a measure of the average molecular weight (or chain length) of all the fatty acids present. As most of the mass of a fat/triester is in the 3 fatty acids, it allows for comparison of the average fatty acid chain length. The long chain fatty acids found in fats have low Saponification value because they have a relatively fewer number of carboxylic functional groups per unit mass of the fat as compared to short chain fatty acids.

Reactions:

$$CH_2OOCC_{17}H_{35}$$
$$|$$
$$CHOOCC_{17}H_{35} + 3KOH ------\rightarrow CHOH + 3C_{17}H_{35}COOK$$
$$|$$
$$CH_2OOC_{17}H_{35}$$

with products:

$$CH_2OH$$
$$|$$
$$CHOH$$
$$|$$
$$CH_2OH$$

Fat

Stearic acid glycerol potassium steareate

The Acid Value of oil is defined as the number of milligrams of potassium hydroxide required to neutralize the free acid present in 1 gram of the oil.The presence of mineral acids in oil is so rare that it is almost unnecessary to look for it, unless the oil is refined in a faulty manner. But, Free organic acids or acidic bodies are always found in Oil, whether they be pure mineral oils or compounded oils with fatty oils.Mineral oils (petroleum oil) are contaminated by mineral acids due to improper refining. In unused refined petroleum oils, the quantity is invariably negligible. Since animal & vegetable oils are the esters of higher fatty acids which on hydrolysis forms organic acids. Hence animal and vegetable oils are generally contaminated by organic acids.Acid present in lubricating oil should be determined because this acid may cause corrosion of equipment. In good lubricating oil the acid value should be less than 0.1 (<0.1). Increase in acid Value taken as an indicator of oxidation of the oil and may lead to formation of gum and sludge which spoils the lubrication process. The Acid Value of fatty oils may vary from 0.2 to 50 and it shows the extent of hydrolysis of glycerol ester of the oil.

Reaction:

$$C_{17}H_{35}COOH + KOH \longrightarrow C_{17}H_{35}COOK + H_2O$$

Regents required

    (1) Oxalic acid solution (2) KOH solution (3) Oil sample (4) Neutral ethyl alcohol (5) Phenolphthalein indicator

Procedure

Part-I: Standardization of KOH Solution

Take 10 ml of oxalic acid solution in conical flask. Add few drops of phenolphthalein indicator. Titrate this solution with KOH solution from burette till colour changes from colourless to light pink. Note the end point as V_2.

Part-II: - Determination of Acid value of Solution

Weight out accurately about 5 g. of the oil under test into a 250 ml conical flask and add 50 ml of neutral alcohol. Heat the flask over a water bath for about 30 minutes. Cool the flask and the contents to room temperature and add a few drops of phenolphthalein indicator. Titrate with the KOH solution until a faint permanent pink color appears at the end point as V2'.

Part-III: - Blank titration

Repeat the same procedure without taking lubricating oil.

Calculations:

Part-I: Standardization of KOH Solution

$N_1V_1 = N_2V_2$

Normality of KOH (N_2) = N_1V_1/V_2

Part II: Determination of acid value of the solution

Acid Value $= N_2 \times V_2 \times$ Eqv. wt of KOH / Weight of the oil taken in gm

Result: The Acid Value of the given oil is found to be_____.

Experiment 15

Determine the heat of neutralization of strong acid with strong base.

Requirements: Thermos flask, glass stirrer, thermometer, stop watch, beaker, measuring cylinder (50cm3), Sodium hydroxide = (0.5 M), Hydrochloric acid = (0.5 M)

Principle:

The heat of neutralization of an acid at a given temperature is defined as the amount of heat evolved when one-gram equivalent of an acid is neutralized by one-gram equivalent of a base in dilute solution at that temperature. It is found that heat of neutralization for all the strong acids and strong base is practically a constant quantity. This can be explained on the basis of theory of ionization. Strong acids and strong bases are assumed to be completely ionized in dilute solutions. Moreover the salts they form on mixing are also completely ionized in dilute aqueous solution. The reaction between a strong acid like HCl and a strong base like NaOH can be written as:

$$H^+_{(aq)} + Cl^-_{(aq)} + Na^+_{(aq)} + OH^-_{(aq)} \longrightarrow Na^+_{(aq)} + Cl^-_{(aq)} + H_2O_{(1)} \quad \Delta H = -57.3 \text{ kJ}$$

or

$$H^+_{(aq)} + OH^-_{(aq)} \longrightarrow H_2O_{(1)} \qquad\qquad \Delta H = -57.3 \text{ kJ}$$

Thus Neutralization is simply a reaction between the H+ions given by the acid and OHions given by the base. In case of strong acids and strong bases the number of H+ions and OHions produced by one gram of any strong acid or strong base is always the same.

Hence the enthalpy of neutralization of a strong acid with a strong base is always the same. A known volume of HCl solution of known concentration is allowed to react completely with a strong alkali in dilute solution. The rise in temperature is noted. Knowing the heat capacity of the calorimeter, masses of acid and base and; their specific heats in dilute solutions, the heat of neutralization can be calculated.

ΔH = -[Heat gained by the calorimeter + Heat gained by the solution]

Procedure:

1. Take a thermos flask and determine its heat capacity.

2. Now take 50cm of HCl in this thermos flask and note down the temperature reading after every half-minute for five minutes.

3. Similarly take 50cm of NaOH in the thermos flask after removing the acid in a beaker. Note down the temperature of NaOH every half-minute for five minutes.

4. Pour the HCl solution in the NaOH already placed in the thermos flask and note down the time of mixing accurately.

5. Note the temperature of the mixture after every half a minute for five minutes.

6. Record the observations as given below.

Observation:

Molarity of the acid = 0.5M

Molarity of the base = 0.5 M

Volume of the acid taken = 50 cm

Volume of the base taken = 50 cm

Time (Sec.)	Temperature °C		Time (Sec.)	Temperature °C
	Acid	Base		

Calculations:

Plot a graph between temperature and time (as shown in the Fig.1)

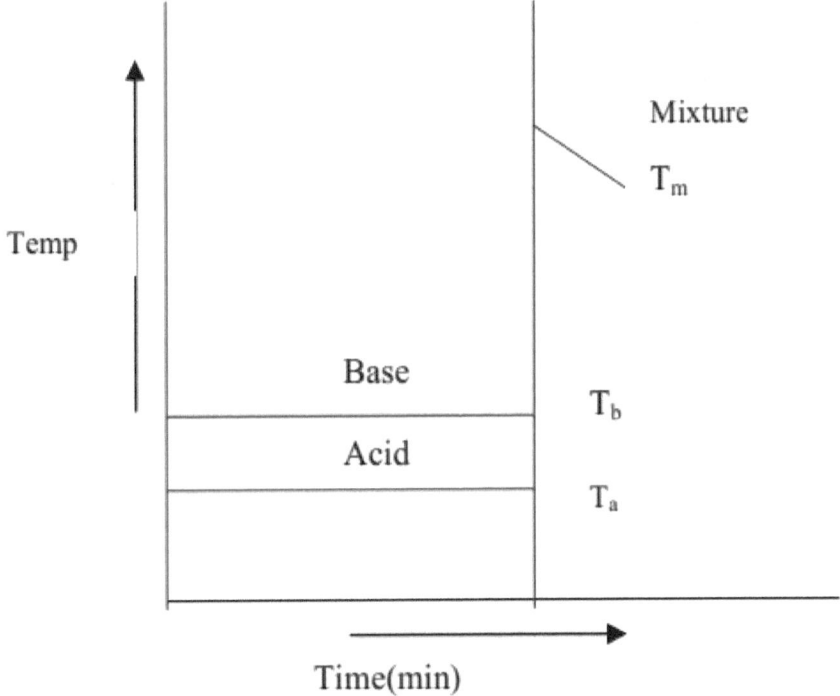

Time(min)

From the Fig1., calculate, T a' Tb, Tm 'at the time of mixing.

Where,

Ta= Temperature of the acid at the time of mixing

Tb = Temperature of the base at the time of mixing

Tm= Temperature of the mixture at the time of mixing

This can be done by drawing a vertical line at the time of mixing. Extend the curves to this vertical line. The points of intersection will give the respective temperatures.

The heat evolved during neutralization will raise the temperature of the solution and that

of thermos flask, i.e.

ΔH = -[Heat gained by the calorimeter + Heat gained by the solution]

   = -[Cp(Calorimeter) (Tm-Tb) + [Cp(Base) (Tm-Tb)] + [Cp(acid)(Tm-Ta)]

   = -[Cp(Calorimeter) (Tm -Tb)] + [V base x specific heat of the base x (Tm -Tb)] + [V_{acid} x specific heat of the acid x (Tm-Ta)]

In the case of dilute solutions, the specific heat of the acid and base can be taken as that of water = 4.185 JK^{-1}

Hence,

Specific heat of water = specific heat of acid = specific heat of base = s

Thus, ΔH = -[Cp(calorimeter) (Tm-Tb) + V bases. (Tm-Tb) + Vacid.s. (Tm-Ta)

Substituting the values of Cp calorimeter' specific heat of water, V_{base} 'V_{acid} Tm, Ta and Tb calculate ΔH . (5 = 4.185 J/g/OC) This is the enthalpy when 50 cm^3 of 0.5 M HCl is neutralized by 50 $cm^3$of 0.5 NaOH.

Number of moles in 50 cm^3 of 0.5M HCl = 0.5/1000 x 50 = 0.025 moles

. ΔH for the neutralization of 1 mole of HCl = $-\Delta H$ /0.025= …………..J mole-l

Result: The heat of neutralization of hydrochloric acid with sodium hydroxide is……………………………. …J mol-l

.**Experiment 16**

Iodometric determination of Copper in given solution

Introduction

When an excess of KI is added to the solution containing Cu^{2+} in neutral or slightly acidic medium, quantitative liberation of iodine takes place.

$$2CuSO_4.5H_2O + 4KI \rightarrow 2CuI2 + 2K_2SO_4 + 5H_2O$$

$$2CuI_2 \rightarrow Cu_2I_2 + I_2$$

This liberated iodine is then titrated against standard Na2S2O3 solution using starch solution as indicator near the end point.

$$2Na_2S_2O_3 + I_2 \rightarrow Na_2S_4O_6 + 2NaI$$

Ionic equation will be: $2Cu^{2+} + 2I^- \rightarrow Cu_2^{2+} + I_2 + 2e^-$

$$I_2 + 2S_2O_3{}^{2-} + 2e^- \rightarrow S_4O_6{}^{2-} + 2I^-$$

From the above equation it is evident that $2Cu^{2+} \equiv I_2 \equiv 2S_2O_2{}^{2-} \equiv 2e^-$

The equivalent weight of Cu^{2+} will be one half of twice the molecular weight since the reaction involves two electrons per two moles of Cu2+

Eq. wt. of Cu^{2+} = (2 x 63.5) / 2 = 63.5

The titration fails when any mineral acid is present in the solution and therefore before commencing the titration the acid should be neutralized. This is done by dropwise addition of NH_4OH until a slight blue precipitate just appears

$$H^+ + OH^- \rightarrow H_2O$$

$$2NH_4OH + Cu^{2+} \rightarrow 2NH_4{}^+ + Cu(OH)_2$$

blue precipitate

The precipitate can be removed by addition of CH_3COOH in the solution. $Cu(OH)_2 + 2CH_3COOH \rightarrow Cu^{2+} + 2CH_3COO- + 2H_2O$

Moreover, the precipitate of Cu_2I_2 absorbs I_2 from the solution and releases it slowly making the detection of sharp end point difficult. So, a small amount of NH_4SCN is added near the end point to displace the absorbed iodine from Cu2I2 precipitate.

Apparatus: Burette, pipette, beakers, conical flask, burette stand and clamp. Chemicals: $K_2Cr_2O_7$, $Na_2S_2O_3.5H_2O$, $CuSO_4.5H_2O$, $NaHCO_3$, KI, NH_4OH, CH_3COOH, starch, NH_4SCN, HCl.

Procedure: 1. Standard K2Cr2O7 solution (0.1 N) is provided.

2. Sodium thiosulphate and copper sulphate solution of unknown strength were supplied.

3. Standardization of sodium thiosulphate ($Na_2S_2O_3$) solution with standard $K_2Cr_2O_7$ solution − Take 40 mL of water in a 250 mL conical flask. To that add 20 mL of potassium iodide (KI) solution (10%) and 1 g of sodium bicarbonate ($NaHCO_3$). Add 6 mL of concentrated hydrochloric acid (HCl) to the above solution and finally add 20 mL of standard $K_2Cr_2O_7$ solution using a pipette. Shake the flask and keep it covered with watch glass in dark for 3–5 minutes. Titrate the liberated iodine with $Na_2S_2O_3$ solution taken in burette. When the colour of the solution fades to straw yellow, add few drops of starch solution and continue the titration till the colour of the solution changes from deep blue to bluish green. Repeat the titration three times. 4. Estimation of copper − Pipette out 20 mL of solution in a 250 mL conical flask and neutralized the solution by drop wise addition of ammonium hydroxide

(NH_4OH) solution (1:1) until a blue precipitate appears. Dissolve the precipitate in acetic acid (CH_3COOH) adding about 0.5 mL in excess. Dilute the solution to about 80 mL and add 20 mL of potassium iodide solution (10%). Keep the flask covered with watch glass in a dark and cool place for about 3–5 minutes and titrate the liberated iodine with standard sodium thiosulphate solution form burette. When the colour of the solution fades to a light yellow, add few drops of starch followed by 20 mL of ammonium thiocyanate (NH_4SCN) solution (10%). Titrate the solution till the blue colour discharges and a white or flesh white residue is left in the flask. Repeat the titration three times.

Observations:

Table 1 – Standardization of $Na_2S_2O_3$ solution with standard $K_2Cr_2O_7$ solution Strength of $K_2Cr_2O_7$ solution = 0.1(N)

S No	Volume of $K_2Cr_2O_7$ solution (ml)	Burette reading (mL)		Volume of $Na_2S_2O_3$ solution (ml)
		Initial	Final	

Table 2 – Estimation of copper using standard $Na_2S_2O_3$ solution

S No	Volume of copper solution (mL)	Burette reading (mL)		Volume of $Na_2S_2O_3$ solution (ml)
		Initial	Final	

Calculations:

A: Standardization of $Na_2S_2O_3$ solution with standard $K_2Cr_2O_7$ solution

$$V_1 \times S_1 = V_2 \times S_2$$

$$S_2 = (V_1 \times S_1) / V_2$$

V1 = Volume of $K_2Cr_2O_7$ solution (0.1 N)

V2 = Volume of $Na_2S_2O_3$ solution

S1 = Strength of $K_2Cr_2O_7$ solution (20 mL)

S2 = Strength of $Na_2S_2O_3$ solution

B Estimation of copper

1000 mL of 1(N) $Na_2S_2O_3$ solution = 63.5 g of copper 1 mL of 1(N) $Na_2S_2O_3$ solution = 0.0635 g of copper Y mL of Z(N) $Na_2S_2O_3$ solution = (0.0635 x Y x Z) g of copper Y = Volume of N $Na_2S_2O_3$ solution required for the titration of the given copper solution (Table 2) Z = Strength of $Na_2S_2O_3$ solution

20 mL solution contains (0.0635 x Y x Z) g of copper 1000 mL solution contains [(0.0635 x Y x Z x 1000) / 20] g of copper = P g (say) of copper

Conclusion: The amount of copper in the given solution is...... P g/L

Precautions:

1. $Na_2S_2O_3$ solution is always taken in the burette in iodometric titrations.

 2. Sufficient amount of KI solution is to be added.

3. The indicator, starch, should be added just before the end point.

4. NH_4SCN solution should be added near the end point to displace the adsorbed iodine and to get a sharp end point.

Experiment 17

Determination of the concentration of iron in water sample by using spectrophotometer

Introduction

Any solution which is colored or can be made to be colored by adding a complexing agent can be analyzed using a spectrophotometer. Solutions containing iron ions are colorless but, with the addition of ortho-phenanthroline, the iron (II) ions in the sample are immediately complexed to produce a species which is orange in color. More iron (II) ions in a sample will result in a deeper orange color. From data obtained from a series of iron (II) standards, it is possible to be able to determine the amount of iron in an unknown sample.

Procedure:

Part I: preparation of standards (steps 1 and 2 may have been done by the instructor)

1. Dissolve 0.7022 grams of ferrous ammonium sulfate, hexahydrate in distilled water. Dilute to 1.00 L. This solution is 100 mg/L Fe +2 (same as 100 ppm).

2. Prepare standard solutions of 0.0, 2.0, 4.0, 6.0, and 8.0 ppm by respectively diluting 0.0, 2.0, 4.0, 6.0, and 8.0 mL of the 100 ppm stock solution into five separate 100.0 mL volumetric flasks. To each flask add 5 mL of a 0.25% ortho-phenanthrolinesolution. Dilute with deionized water to 100.0 mL.

3. Clean and dry a set of cuvets.

4. Label the cuvets blank, 2 ppm, 4ppm, 6 ppm, 8 ppm.

5. Fill each cuvet with the appropriate solution.
   Part II: Preparation of the unknown
1. Obtain an unknown sample from the instructor or prepare your own unknown using a collected water sample.

2. If using a collected water sample, add 5 mL of the 0.25% ortho-phenanthroline solution to a 100.00 mL volumetric flask. Dilute to mark with collected water sample.

   Part III: forming the standard curve
1. Turn on the spectrophotometer. Press the **A/T/C** button on the Spec select absorbance.

2. Adjust the wavelength to **510** nm by pressing the **nm** arrow up or down.

3. Insert the blank into the cell holder and close the door. Position the cell so that the light passes through clear walls.

4. Press **0 ABS/100% T** to set the blank to 0 absobance.

5. Record the absorbance of the 0ppm solution. Obtain absorbance readings for each of the other standard solutions.

6. If using a collected water sample as an unknown, use collected water without the 0.25% ortho- phenanthroline solution as the blank and re-zero the absorbance. If not, procede to the next step.

7. Obtain an absorbance reading for the unknown sample.

8. Make a graph of Concentration (x-axis) vs. absorbance (y-axis).

9. From the standard curve, determine the concentration of iron in this unknown sample.

Table 1:

Concentration	Absorbance
Blank	
2.0 ppm	
4.0 ppm	
6.0 ppm	
8.0 ppm	
Sample 1	
Sample2	

Result: The unknown water sample contains iron ....

Questions:

1. Explain why it was necessary to add ortho-phenanthroline to the solutions.
2. What is the purpose of preparing and analyzing standard iron solutions?
3. What other items could be analyzed using this method?

Experiment 18

Proximate analysis of a sample of coal

PRINCIPLE

The proximal analysis, which includes the determination of moisture, volatile matter, ash and fixed carbon this give quick and valuable information regarding for commercial and industrial use.

PROCEDURE -

1. Moisture – It is determined by heating a known quantity of air dried coal from 1050C-1100C for one hour and calculating the loss in weight as percentage. Heat a silica crucible with lid, cool it in a desiccator and weigh. Take 1 gram of coal sample in it and again weigh, heat the crucible without lid in an air oven at 1050C-1100C for 1 hour, cool the crucible in a desiccator and weigh it again. The loss of weight corresponds to the moisture.

2. Volatile Matter:- It is determined by heating 1 gram of air dried coal for 1 minute in a translucent silica crucible at a steady temperature of 9250C in a muffle furnace.

3. Ash :- Take one gram of powdered air dried sample in previously weighed crucible having 5 cm diameter and 1 cm depth. Place a crucible on a claypipe triangle and heat over a Bunsen burner with a wavy flame. Place the crucible without lid in muffle furnace at 7500C and heat for 1 hour cool it in a desiccators to room temperature and weigh with lid.

4. Fixed carbon :- The sum of total of percentages of volatile matter, moisture and ash subtracted from 100 gives the percentage of fixed carbon.

CALCULATION:-

1. Moisture –

Weight of empty crucible = W1 gm

Weight of crucible + sample = W2 gm

Weight of crucible + sample after heating = W3 gm

$$\% \text{ moisture} = \frac{W_2 - W_3}{W_2 - W_1} \times 100$$

2. Volatile matter –

Weight of empty crucible = W4 gm

Weight of crucible + sample = W5 gm

Weight of crucible + sample after heating = W6 gm

$$\% \text{ (moisture + Volatile matter)} = \frac{W_5 - W_6}{W_5 - W_4} \times 100$$

$$\% \text{ of Volatile matter} = \left(\frac{W_5 - W_6}{W_5 - W_4} \times 100 \right) + (\% \text{ moisture})$$

3. Ash –

Weight of empty crucible = W7 gm

Weight of crucible + sample = W8 gm

Weight of crucible + ash = W9 gm

$$\% \text{ Ash} = \frac{W_9 - W_8}{W_8 - W_7} \times 100$$

4. Fixed carbon :-% Fc = 100 – (% Moisture + % Volatile matter + % Ash)

Experiment 19

To determine melting point and boiling point of unknown compounds.

Introduction

The melting point of a compound is the temperature at which the solid phase is in equilibrium with the liquid phase. A solid compound changes to a liquid when the molecules acquire enough energy to overcome the forces holding them together in an orderly crystalline lattice. For most organic compounds, these intermolecular forces are relatively weak. The melting point range is defined as the span of temperature from the point at which the crystals first begin to liquefy to the point at which the entire sample is liquid. Most pure organic compounds melt over a narrow temperature range of 1-2 °C. The presence of a soluble impurity almost always causes a decrease in the melting point expected for the pure compound and a broadening of the melting point range. In order to understand the effects of impurities on melting point behavior, consider the melting point-mass percent composition diagram for two different fictitious organic compounds, X and Y, shown in Figure 1. The vertical axis represents temperature and the horizontal axis represents varying mass percent compositions of X and Y.

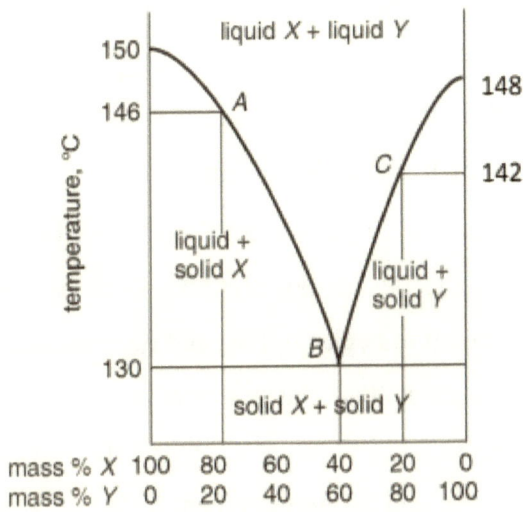

Figure 1. Melting point-mass percent composition diagram

Both compounds have sharp melting points.

Compound X melts at 150 °C, as shown on the left vertical axis, and Y melts at 148 °C, as shown on the right vertical axis. As compound X is added to pure Y, the melting point of the mixture decreases along curve C-B until a minimum temperature of 130 °C is reached. Point B corresponds to 40 mass percent X and 60 mass percent Y and is called the eutectic composition for compound X and Y. Here, both solid X and solid Y are in equilibrium with the liquid. The eutectic temperature of 130 °C is the lowest possible melting point for a mixture of X and Y. At temperatures below 130 °C, mixtures of X and Y exist together only in solid form. Consider a 100-μg mixture composed of 20 μg of X and 80 μg of Y. In this mixture, X acts as an impurity in Y. As the mixture is heated, the temperature rises to the eutectic temperature of 130 °C. At this temperature, X and Y begin to melt together at point B, the eutectic composition of 40 mass percent X and 60 percent Y. The temperature remains constant at 130 °C until all 20 µg of X melts. At the eutectic temperature, X and Y will melt in the ratio of 40 parts X to 60 parts Y. If 20 µg of X melts, then 30 µg of Y also melts (20 µg X x 60/40 ratio = 30 µg Y). At this point, the remaining 50 µg of solid Y is in equilibrium with a molten mixture of the eutectic composition. As more heat is applied to the mixture, the temperature begins to rise, and the remaining Y begins to melt. Y continues to melt as the temperature increases, shown by curve B-C. Finally, at 142 °C, point C, where the liquid composition is 20 mass percent X and 80 mass percent Y, all of Y is melted. At temperatures higher than 142 °C, liquid X and liquid Y exist together with a composition at which the entire mixture liquefies is 142 °C, 6 degrees lower than the melting point of pure Y. Also, the melting point range 130-142 °C is quite broad. If a mixture has exactly the eutectic composition of 40 mass percent X and 60 mass percent Y, the mixture shows a sharp melting point at 130 °C. Observing this melting point could lead to the false conclusion that the mixture is a pure compound. Addition of either pure X or pure Y to the mixture causes an increase in the melting point, as indicated by curve B-A or B-C, respectively. Observing this melting point increase indicates that the original sample is not pure. Because the melting point of a compound is a physical constant, the melting point can be helpful in determining the identity of an unknown compound. A good correlation between the experimentally measured melting point of an unknown compound and the accepted melting point of a known compound suggests that the compound may be the same. However, many different compounds have the same melting point.

A mixed melting point can be useful in confirming the identity of an unknown compound. A small portion of a known compound, whose melting point is known from the chemical literature, is mixed with the unknown compound. If the melting point of the mixture is the same as that of the known compound, then the known and the unknown compounds may be identical. A decrease in the melting point of the mixture and a broadening of the melting point range indicates that the compounds are likely to be different. Melting points can also be used to assess compound purity. Generally, a melting point range of 5 °C or more indicates that a compound is impure. Purification of the compound causes the melting point range to narrow and the melting point to increase. Repeated purification may be necessary before the melting point range narrows to 1-2 °C and reaches its maximum value, indicating that the compound is pure. In practice, measuring the melting point of a crystalline compound involves several steps. First, a finely powdered compound is packed into a melting point capillary tube to a depth of 1-2 mm. Then the capillary tube containing the sample compound is inserted into the melting point apparatus. If the melting point of the compound is unknown, it is convenient to first measure the approximate melting point of the compound, called the orientation melting point. The sample is heated at a rate of 10-15 °C per minute until it melts. Then the melting point apparatus is cooled to approximately 15 °C below the orientation melting point. A new sample is heated, increasing the temperature at a much slower rate of 1-2 °C per minute, to accurately measure the melting point. A slow heating rate is necessary because heating a sample too rapidly may cause the thermometer reading to differ from the actual temperature of the heat source. If the melting point of the sample is known, the sample can be quickly heated to within 10- 15 °C of its melting point. Then the heating rate can be slowed to increase 1-2 °C per minute until the sample melts. Errors in observed melting points often occur due to a poor heat transfer rate from the heat source to the compound. One cause of poor heat transfer rate is the placement of too much sample into the capillary tube. Finely ground particles of the compound are also necessary for good heat transfer. If the particles are too coarse, they do not pack well, causing air pockets that slow heat transfer. Sometimes slight changes, such as shrinking and sagging, occur in the crystalline structure of the sample before melting occur. Also, traces of solvent may be present due to insufficient drying and may appear as droplets on the outside surface of the sample. This phenomenon is called sweating and should not be mistaken for melting. The initial melting point temperature always corresponds to the first appearance of liquid within the bulk of the sample itself. Some compounds decompose at or near their melting points. This decomposition is usually characterized by a darkening in the color of the compound as it melts. If the decomposition and melting occur over a narrow temperature range of 1-2 °C, the melting point is used for identification and as an indication of sample purity. The melting point of such compound is listed in the literature accompanied by d or decomp. If the sample melts over a large temperature range with decomposition, the data cannot be used for identification purposes. Some compounds pass directly from solid to vapor phase without going through the liquid phase, a process called sublimation. When sublimation occurs, the sample at the bottom of the capillary tube vaporizes and recrystallizes higher up in the capillary tube. A sealed capillary tube is used to take the melting point of a compound that sublimes at or below its melting point. The literature reports the melting point for these compounds accompanied by s, sub, or subl. Boiling points are also useful physical properties for indicating the purity of an organic compound. Boiling point is the temperature at which the vapor pressure of a liquid equals atmospheric pressure or some other applied pressure. A boiling point is commonly measured during a distillation, in which a liquid is heated to form vapor, and then the vapor is condensed and collected in another container. The boiling temperature is measured as distillation vapor covers the bulb of a thermometer suspended above the boiling liquid. Typically, the most accurate boiling point measurement is the relatively constant temperature achieved during a distillation.

Experimental Procedure for Melting Point Determination

1) Obtain a sample and put the sample into a capillary tube (about 2-3 mm in height).

2) Measure the melting point using the apparatus as shown in Figure 2. Attach the capillary tube to a thermometer with sewing thread. Place 25-30 mL of paraffin oil or glycerol in a 50 mL beaker.

3) Turn on the hotplate and observe the melting point. Use a clean glass rod to stir the oil to ensure a uniform heat distribution.

4) Record the melting point range (for example 70-73°C). Repeat the experiment one more time.

5 Put the sample into another capillary tube, and measure the melting point of the sample again using the electrothermal melting point apparatus, e.g. as shown in Figure 3. Record the melting point range.

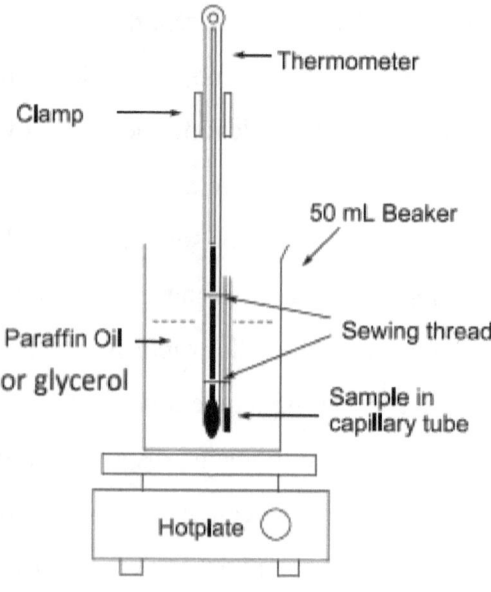

Figure 2. Apparatus set-up for melting-point determination

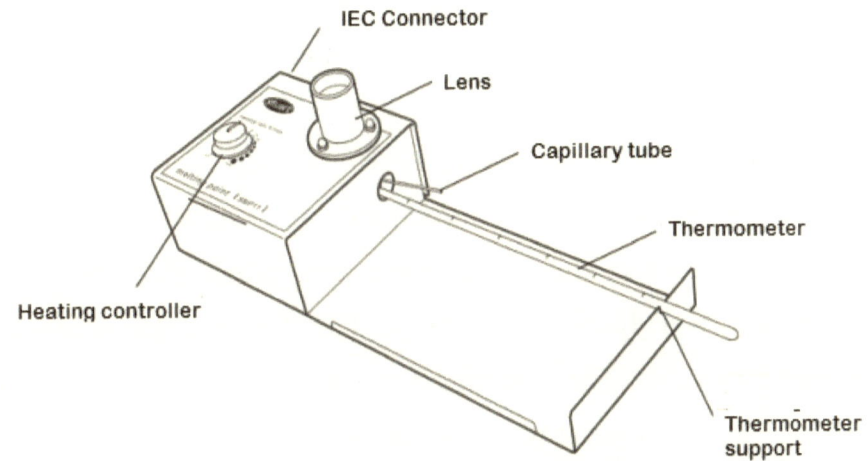

Figure 3 . Example of an electrothermal melting point apparatus
Based on the observed melting points, select 2 compounds in the table below that are most likely to be your unknown

Compound	M. P. (°C)
Resorcinol	110-112
Acetanilide	113-116
Citric acid	153-159
Salicylic acid	158-161
Oxalic acid	99-101

8) Verify the identity of your unknown by measuring the mixed melting point with each of the selected known compounds using either of the methods mentioned earlier. The mixture can be made by putting together an equal quantity of the unknown and the known compounds on a watch glass. Use a spatula to thoroughly blend the mixture. Record the melting point range and identify the unknown compounds

Experiment 20

To estimate saponification value of a given oil sample

Introduction

The saponification value of oil is the number of milligrams of potassium hydroxide required to saponify one gram of the oil or fat under the specified conditions. The vegetables or animal oils are esters of fatty acids and glycerol. They react with KOH to form the potassium salts of fatty acids. The saponification value of oil is determined by refluxing a known quantity of the sample with a known excess of standard KOH solution and determining the alkali consumed by titrating the unreacted alkali. It is a measure of the average molecular weight (or chain length) of all the fatty acids present. As most of the mass of a fat/triester is in the 3 fatty acids, it

allows for comparison of the average fatty acid chain length. The long chain fatty acids found in fats have low Saponification value because they have a relatively fewer number of carboxylic functional groups per unit mass of the fat as compared to short chain fatty acids

Reactions

$$
\begin{array}{l}
CH_2OOCC_{17}H_{35} \\
\quad | \\
CHOOCC_{17}H_{35} + 3KOH \longrightarrow \\
\quad | \\
CH_2OOC_{17}H_{35}
\end{array}
\qquad
\begin{array}{l}
CH_2OH \\
\quad | \\
CHOH + 3C_{17}H_{35}COOK \\
\quad | \\
CH_2OH
\end{array}
$$

Fat

Stearic acid glycerol potassium steareate

The Acid Value of oil is defined as the number of milligrams of potassium hydroxide required to neutralize the free acid present in 1 gram of the oil. The presence of mineral acids in oil is so rare that it is almost unnecessary to look for it, unless the oil is refined in a faulty manner. But, Free organic acids or acidic bodies are always found in Oil, whether they be pure mineral oils or compounded oils with fatty oils. Mineral oils (petroleum oil) are contaminated by mineral acids due to improper refining. In unused refined petroleum oils, the quantity is invariably negligible. Since animal & vegetable oils are the esters of higher fatty acids which on hydrolysis forms organic acids. Hence animal and vegetable oils are generally contaminated by organic acids.

Acid present in lubricating oil should be determined because this acid may cause corrosion of equipment. In good lubricating oil the acid value should be less than 0.1 (<0.1). Increase in acid Value taken as an indicator of oxidation of the oil and may lead to formation of gum and sludge which spoils the lubrication process. The Acid Value of fatty oils may vary from 0.2 to 50 and it shows the extent of hydrolysis of glycerol ester of the oil.

Reaction:

$C_{17}H_{35}COOH+KOH \text{ ----------------} > C_{17}H_{35}COOK+H2O$

Regents required:

(1) Oxalic acid solution (2) KOH solution (3) Oil sample (4) Neutral ethyl alcohol   (5) Phenolphthalein indicator.

Procedure:

Part-I: Standardization of KOH Solution

Take 10 ml of oxalic acid solution in conical flask. Add few drops of phenolphthalein indicator. Titrate this solut ion with KOH solution from burette till colour changes from colourless to light pink. Note the end point as V2.

Part-II: - Determination of Acid value of Solution

Weight out accurately about 5 g. of the oil under test into a 250 ml conical flask and add 50 ml of neutral alcohol. Heat the flask over a water bath for about 30 minutes. Cool the flask and the contents to room temperature and add a few drops of phenolphthalein indicator. Titrate with the KOH solution until a faint permanent pink color appears at the end point as V_2'.

Part-III: - Blank titration

Repeat the same procedure without taking lubricating oil.

Calculations:

Part-I: Standardization of KOH Solution

Std Oxalic acid   Vs   KOH

$$N_1V_1 = N_2V_2$$

Normality of KOH

$$N_2 = \frac{N_1V_1}{V_2}$$

Part-II: - Determination of Acid value of Solution

$$\text{Acid value} = \frac{\text{Normality of KOH} \times V_2 \times \text{eq. wt. of KOH}}{\text{Weight of the oil taken in g}}$$

Result: The Acid Value of the given oil is found to be_____.

Experiment 21

To study the nature of corrosion of several metals in gel medium

Introduction

Spontaneously redox reaction in electrochemistry cell is the sum of two half reaction cell with positive value of total electromotive force cell, emf. The level of corrosion of metal is studied by comparing oxidation level relative to O2 in water. In base condition, reduction of oxygen in water yield to OH- ion, which forms pink-red color with phenolphthalein (pp) indicator. Iron oxidized to Fe2+ which form blue color with ferricyanide ion. If such redox reactions take place in gel medium, the resulted-color localized in oxidation or reduction area. Due to the slow spreading of ions, it is possible to identify anode and cathode side. The active site of iron stick (such as iron nail), found at the end of nail. The electrons flow trough the stick and then captured by oxygen. Therefore, oxidation occurred at the end of nail, and reduction at the center

Materials

Test tube   - $K_3[Fe(CN)_6]$ solution
Beaker glass 250 mL   - Gel
Bunsen burner, wire gauze - Phenolphthalein (pp)
Iron nail   - Zink sheet
Aluminum sheet   - Tin sheet
        - Copper sheet

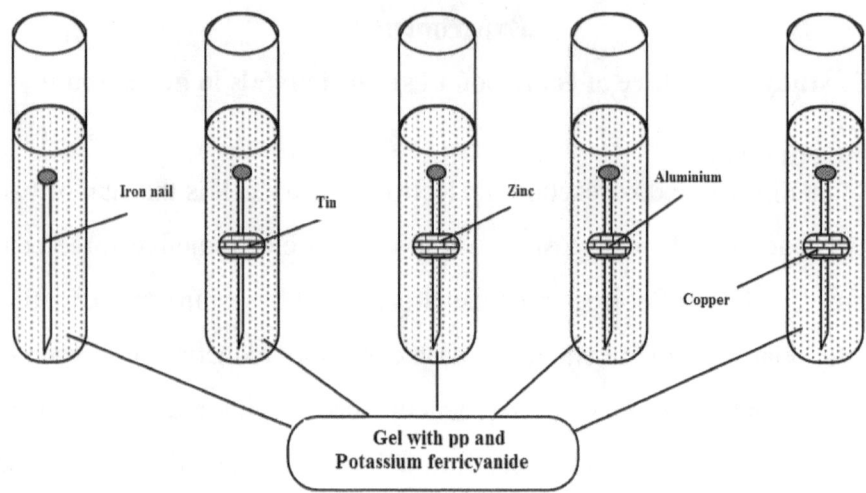

Figure 1 Experiment design

Procedure
A. Seaweed gel making

1. Boil 80 mL of aquadest in beaker glass 250 mL.

2. Pour 0.5 g seaweed into aquadest and stir it until the gel dissolved.

3. Add 5 g of NaCl into the solution and stir continuously

4. Add 2 mL of phenolphthalein (pp) indicator and 1 mL of 0.1 M K [Fe(CN) 3 6] solution. Stir until homogeny and stop the heating. Cool down the gel. The color of the mixture must be yellow, not green, blue or uncolored

B. Cleaning of iron nail

5. Submerge five iron nails into 15 mL of 2 M H SO 2 4 solution in the test tube for five minutes.

6. Boil 50 mL of water in beaker glass 250 mL, clean the acid from the nail carefully (on step 5), rinse nails with water and then put the nails gently into boiling water. Move the nails into test tube with clean pliers.

C. Working with cleaned nails

7.   Label test tubes 1 to 5. Place a cleaned nail into test tube 1. Attention: for test tube 2 – 5, nails must be precisely fit the hole of metals (Figure1)

8.   Make a hole on copper sheet, zinc, tin and aluminum sheet with a nail. Put a cleaned nail through those holes. Ensure, there is a good contact between the two metals

9.   Place those pairs of metals in the test tube 2 – 5. Pour gel indicator gently into test tube 1 – 5. Attention: there must no bubble.

10. Place the test tubes on a shelf tube. After a while, observe the color changing around gel. According to the observation, color the area around nail and metal sheet on Figure 1

Result

The amount of flowing electricity: ………………….. mA

Sketch the experiment design and show the color changing on each electrode.

Write the anodic (oxidation) and cathodic (reduction) reaction.

Cathodic reaction :

……………………………………………………………………………

Anodic reaction :

……………………………………………………………………………

Experiment 22

To study the corrosion character of metals (iron and copper)

Introduction

The amount of electron transferred during corrosion process measured by using multimeter. The function of electrodes (anode species and cathode species) confirmed by knowing the direction of electron flowing or potential gap. Sodium chloride acts as electrolyte to keep ions mobility.

Materials

Iron sheet 8 cm x 2 cm   - 0.1 M $K_3[Fe(CN)_6]$ solution

Copper sheet 8 cm x 2 cm - Phenolphthalein (pp)

Sandpaper   - 3% NaCl solution

Multimeter or milliammeter   - Acetone

Procedure

1. Clean the iron and copper sheets with sandpaper and acetone soaked-cotton to clean the fat.

2. Mix the solutions of 40 mL of 3 % NaCl solution and 20 mL of 0.1 - 0.1 M $K_3[Fe(CN)_6]$ solution in beaker glass 250 mL to make feroxyl indicator. Add phenolphthalein indicator gently into the mixture and stir it. In this experiment, feroxyl indicator produces blue color with Fe2+ ion and pp produce pink color with OH- ion.

3. Place an iron sheet and a cooper sheet into white paper based-beaker glass 250 mL. By using alligator clips, connect the two metals with milliammeter. Pour the feroxyl solution into the beaker glass until the electrode ends immersed.

4. Observe the electricity current indicator on milliammeter to investigate the amount electrons flow through the two metals and the color changing. When the color changed, observe the indicator on milliammeter.

5. Record the result of the observation on worksheet

Result

The amount of flowing electricity current (Fe and Cu): ……………..mA

Based on the observation, conclude metals that act as anode (oxidation) and cathode (reduction)

Write the anodic (oxidation) and cathodic (reduction) reaction.

Cathodic reaction:

………………………………………………………………….

Anodic reaction :

………………………………………………………………….

References

1   Roussak, Oleg, Gesser, H. D.,A Applied Chemistry-Textbook for Engineers and Technologists, Springer, 2013, ISBN 978-1-4614-4262-2

2   A Text Book Of Engineering Chemistry, Shashi Chawla, Dhanpat Rai & Co. India

3   Engineering Chemistry Kushal Qanungo PHI Learning Private Limited ISBN: 9788120338180, 2009

4   Applied Chemistry (Including Lab Manual), Pooja Sharma, Vayu Education of India, 2015

5   Applied Chemistry : Theory and Practice , O.P. Vermani, New Age International India 2005

6   Applied Chemistry B S Chauhan, Vayu Education of India, 2013, ISBN-10: 938313772X

7   Experiments in Applied Chemistry, Sunita Rattan, S.K. Kataria & Sons; 2011, ISBN-10: 8188458058

8   Experiments in Applied Chemistry, Peter Tooley, (Lincoln, United Kingdom, ISBN 10: 0719526523, 1975

9   Applied Chemistry Practical's, A. Gaddamwar and P. R. Rajput, LAP Lambert Academic Publishing 2013, ISBN-10: 3659408638